SEAFOOD

MASTERY

2 in 1

+100 Fresh & Delicious Recipes to
Maintain a Healthy Weight

Ally Rogers, Jim Morris

Sommario

LOBSTER..12

Lobster Thermidor With Newburg Sauce................13

Maine lobster roll...16

 Stuffed Lobster Thermidor.......................................18

Lobster with Vanilla..22

OCTOPUS...25

Octopus in red wine...26

Pickled octopus 29

Octopus Cooked In Wine...32

Sicilian grilled baby octopus 34

SCALLOPS...36

Seafood Pot Pie..37

Baked Scallops with Garlic Sauce 39

Scallops Provencal..40

 Scallops With White Butter Sauce..........................42

HADDOCK...44

Haddock with Herbed Butter over Caramelized
Onions and Tomatoes..46

Cajun Spiced Haddock...49

Haddock, Leek & Potato Chowder...........................51

Smoked haddock & Tomato Chutney 53

SWORDFISH 56

   Mandarin sesame swordfish 57

   Spicy swordfish steaks..................................60

SALMON..62

   Salmon with grilled onions................................63

   Cedar plank salmon..66

   Smoked garlic salmon 69

   Salmon with tarragon dill cream sauce 72

   Blackened Salmon 75

   Magic baked salmon 78

   Pan-seared salmon with zucchini pesto....................80

   Poached Salmon in Tomato Garlic Broth..................84

   Prosciutto/Salmon Wraps.................................86

   Salmon Pate...90

   Spice-Rubbed Salmon with Sautéed Greens...........92

   Stovetop Smoked Salmon with Dill-Lemon Aioli.....97

   Dill-Lemon Aioli..99

   Soy-Ginger Marinated Salmon 101

   Sweet Salmon with Ginger and Scallions...............104

   Butter Barbecued Salmon 107

   Curried Salmon-Rice Loaf...............................110

   Salmon-Broccoli Loaf with Dill and Capers...........111

Salmon in Vodka Cream Sauce with Green Peppercorns...115

Salmon with Basil Cream Sauce................................118

Salmon with Cumin-Coriander Crema & Chipotle Salsa...121

Spicy Salmon and Eggplant.................................124

Poached Salmon/Sautéed Tuna...........................127

Citrus Salmon...128

Grilled Salmon...132

Thai salmon parcels...133

Smoked Salmon Dip...137

Wild Salmon, Chive& Cheddar Grills....................139

Salmon Burgers...142

Teriyaki Salmon Wrap.......................................145

Salmon with tarragon dill cream sauce...............147

SHRIMP...158

Spicy grilled shrimp...159

Grilled herbed shrimp.......................................162

Shrimp en brochette...165

Shrimp packets...168

Basil shrimp...169

Grilled bacon-wrapped shrimp...........................171

Alabama Shrimp Bake.......................................175

Almost Shrimp Paesano 178

Bean & Shrimp Risotto.................................181

Beer-Broiled Shrimp.................................184

Boiled Gulf Shrimp 185

Rémoulade Sauce 187

California Scampi 190

Champagne Shrimp And Pasta.................................192

Coconut Shrimp with Jalapeño Jelly 195

Coconut Tempura Shrimp.................................197

Cornsicles with Shrimp and Oregano 200

Creamy Pesto Shrimp.................................203

Easy Creamed Shrimp 209

Eggplant Canoes.................................211

Fernandina Shrimp Gravy.................................214

Fried Breaded Shrimp 216

Gambas al Ajillo (Garlic Shrimp) 219

Grilled Marinated Shrimp 221

Texas Shrimp.................................225

Hawaiian shrimp Skewers 227

Honey-Thyme Grilled Shrimp 230

Hot and Spicy Shrimp.................................234

Italian Broiled Shrimp.................................237

Jerk Shrimp with Sweet Jamaican Rice..................240

Killer Shrimp...242

Lemon-Garlic Broiled Shrimp............................245

Lime Pepper Shrimp..248

Louisiana Shrimp Esplanade 249

Malibu Stir Fry Shrimp 253

Outa Sight Shrimp 254

Really Cool Shrimp Salad.................................257

M-80 Rock Shrimp...258

Toast of the Town...262

Shrimp Curry with Mustard 266

Shrimp Curry 268

Shrimp in Garlic Sauce 271

Shrimp in Mustard Cream Sauce.......................274

Gazpacho 278

Shrimp Marinara..283

Shrimp Newburg 287

Spicy Marinated Shrimp 290

Spicy Singapore Shrimp 292

Starlight Shrimp..295

Zesty Alabama Cocktail Sauce 297

Butterfly Shrimp 299

Cajun Shrimp...303

Chilled Aromatic Shrimp with Cilantro-Ginger-Lime
Cream...305

New Orleans BBQ shrimp 308

Curried Corn and Shrimp Soup 311

Fiesta Shrimp 313

 Pasta with Shrimp in Tomato Cream 316

Caribbean Coconut Shrimp..318

Papaya garlic Shrimp..320

Shrimp Creole...322

Shrimp and Grits/Classic Charleston Breakfast
Shrimp..323

Biscuit Topped Seafood Gumbo Pie............................327

Creamy butter shrimp...330

Prosciutto wrapped shrimp 333

Thai peanut shrimp curry..336

Seafood recipes

+50 recetas frescas y deliciosas
para mantener un peso saludable

Jim Morris

All rights reserved.

Disclaimer

LOBSTER

Lobster Thermidor With Newburg Sauce

Sauce

- 3 tablespoons butter
- 1 cup clam juice
- 1/4 to 1/2 cup milk
- 1/2 teaspoon paprika
- Pinch of salt
- 3 tablespoons sherry
- 2 tablespoons all-purpose flour
- 4 tablespoons light cream

Melt butter over a medium low flame. When completely melted, add paprika and stir for 2 minutes. Add the flour to the butter and stir for 2 to 3 minutes to cook the roux. Stir constantly to avoid burning. Add the clam juice and stir until thickening begins. Add 1/4 cup milk, light cream and sherry. Simmer for 5 minutes and, if needed, add remaining 1/4 cup milk.

Lobster

- 5 ounces lobster meat, cut into 1-inch chunks
- 1 tablespoon finely chopped pimentos
- 1/2 cup thick sliced mushrooms
- 1 tablespoon chopped chives

- Butter for sautéing
- 1 tablespoon sherry

Newburg Sauce
- 1/2 to 1 cup grated Cheddar cheese
- Preheat oven to 350 degrees F.

Over medium heat, melt enough butter to lightly cover the bottom of a heavy, large sauté pan. Place the lobster, chives, pimentos and mushrooms in the pan and stir for 3 to 4 minutes. Increase the heat to high and add the sherry to deglaze the pan. Be careful as the sherry may flame up as the alcohol burns off.

Stir in 4 ounces of Newburg Sauce and stir for 1 minute. Pour into a single serving casserole and sprinkle with the cheese. Bake for about 5 minutes or until the cheese has melted and is bubbly.

Maine lobster roll

Four 1- to 1 1/4-pound lobsters

1/4 cup plus 2 tablespoons mayonnaise
Salt and freshly ground pepper
1/4 cup finely diced celery
2 tablespoons fresh lemon juice
Pinch of cayenne pepper
4 top-split hot dog buns
2 tablespoons unsalted butter, melted
1/2 cup shredded Boston lettuce

Prepare a large ice-water bath. In a very large pot of boiling salted water, cook the lobsters until they turn bright red, about 10 minutes. Using tongs, plunge the lobsters into the ice-water bath for 2 minutes, then drain.

Twist off the lobster tails and claws and remove the meat. Remove and discard the intestinal vein that runs the length of each lobster tail. Cut the lobster meat into 1/2-inch pieces and pat dry, then transfer to a strainer set over a bowl and refrigerate until very cold, at least 1 hour.

In a large bowl, mix the lobster meat with the mayonnaise and season with salt and pepper. Fold in the diced celery, lemon juice and cayenne pepper until well blended.

Heat a large skillet. Brush the sides of the hot dog buns with the melted butter and toast over moderate heat until golden brown on both sides. Transfer the hot dog buns to plates, fill them with the shredded lettuce and the lobster salad and serve immediately.

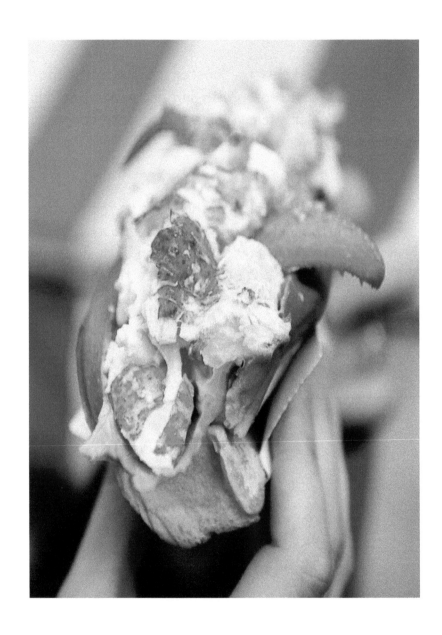

Stuffed Lobster Thermidor

- 6 (1 pound) frozen lobster tails
- 10 tablespoons butter, melted
- 1 cup sliced fresh mushrooms
- 4 tablespoons flour
- 1 teaspoon dry mustard
- 2 dashes ground nutmeg
- 2 dashes cayenne pepper
- 1 teaspoon salt
- 1 cup milk
- 1 cup half-and-half
- 2 egg yolks, slightly beaten
- 1 teaspoon lemon juice
- 2 tablespoons sherry wine
- 1/2 cup fine bread crumbs
- 2 tablespoons grated Parmesan cheese

Preheat oven to 450 degrees F.

Place lobster tails in large pot of boiling water and cover. Cook until tender, about 20 minutes; drain.

Cut each tail in half lengthwise and dice lobster meat. Set aside empty lobster tails.

Pour 1/4 cup butter in saucepan; add mushrooms and sauté until slightly browned. Blend in flour and mix in seasonings. Add milk and half-and-half gradually to mixture, stirring constantly until thick. Add small amount of hot mixture to egg yolks, stirring constantly; then return egg yolk mixture to cream sauce, again stirring constantly and cooking until thickened. Stir in lemon juice, sherry and lobster meat; spoon into lobster shells. Combine bread crumbs, Parmesan cheese and remaining butter; sprinkle over stuffed lobster tails. Place on cookie sheet and bake at 400 degrees F for 15 minutes.

Serves 6.

Lobster with Vanilla

This is a recipe that my (Oz) mother-in-law gave me while we were in Florida. Not sure where she got it, but it's a photocopy of something.

- Live 1 1/2 pound lobster per person
- 1 onion
- 1 clove of garlic
- Tomatoes, skinned and finely chopped
- A little wine or fish stock
- Butter
- Sherry
- Vanilla extract
- Cayenne pepper

Cut the lobster in half. Crack the claws and cut the tail through the joints. Melt a knob of butter in a heavy saute pan, fry the onion and garlic gently. Add the lobster pieces and cook until they go red, before removing them to someplace warm. Now turn up the heat and add the rest of the ingredients, except the vanilla, buter and cayenne. Reduce the tomatoes until they're a bubbling mush, then turn down the heat and add the butter in bits and stir to stop the sauce from separating. Finally, add half a teaspoon of vanilla and a shake of cayenne. Pour the sauce over the lobster and serve with rice.

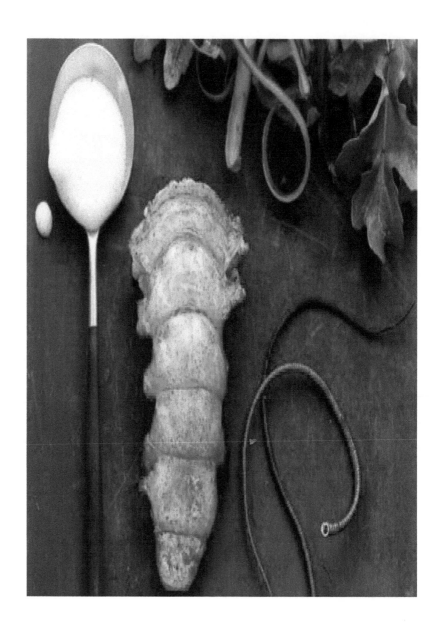

OCTOPUS

Octopus in red wine

INGREDIENTS

- 1kg (2.25lb) young octopus
- 8tbsp olive oil
- 350g (12oz) small onions or shallots 150ml (0.25pint) red wine 6tbsp red wine vinegar
- 225g (8oz) canned tomatoes, roughly chopped 2tbsp tomato puree
- 4 bay leaves
- 2 tsp dried oregano
- black pepper
- 2tbsp chopped parsley

DIRECTIONS

First clean the octopus. Pull off the tentacles, remove and discard the intestines and the ink sac, the eyes and the beak. Skin the octopus and wash and scrub it thoroughly to remove any traces of sand. Cut it into 4-5cm (1.5-2inch) pieces and put it into a saucepan over medium heat to release the liquid. Stir the octopus until this liquid has evaporated. Pour on the oil and stir the octopus to seal it on all sides. Add the whole onions and cook them, stirring once or twice, until they color slightly.

Add the wine, the vinegar, tomatoes, tomato puree, bay leaves, oregano and several grindings of pepper. Stir well, cover the pan and simmer very gently for 1-1.25 hrs., checking from time to time that the sauce has not dried out. If it does - and this would only happen if the heat were too high - add a little more wine or water. The octopus is cooked when it can be easily pierced with a skewer.

The sauce should be thick, like a runny paste. If any of the liquid separates, remove the lid from the pan, slightly increase the heat and stir until some of the liquid evaporates and the sauce thickens. Discard the bay leaves and stir in the parsley. Taste the sauce and adjust the seasoning if necessary. Serve, if you like, with rice and a salad. A Greek essential is country bread to mop up the sauce.

SERVES 4-6

Pickled octopus

Ingredients

1. 1kg (2.25lb) young octopus
2. about 150ml (0.25pint) olive oil
3. about 150ml (0.25pint) red wine vinegar 4 cloves garlic
4. salt and black pepper 4-6 stalks thyme or 1tsp dried thyme lemon wedges, to serve

Directions

Prepare and wash the octopus (as in Octopus in Red Wine). Place the head and tentacles in a pan with 6-8tbsp water, cover and simmer for 1-1.25 hours until it is tender. Test it with a skewer. Drain off any remaining liquid and set aside to cool.

Cut the flesh into 12mm (0.5inch) strips and pack them loosely into a screw-topped jar. Mix enough oil and vinegar to fill the jar - the exact amount will depend on the relative volumes of the seafood and the container - stir in the garlic and season with salt and pepper. If you are using dried thyme, mix it with the liquid at this stage. Pour it over the octopus, making sure that every last piece is completely immersed. If you are using thyme stalks, push them into the jar.

Cover the jar and set it aside for at least 4-5 days before using.

To serve, drain the octopus and serve it on small individual plates or saucers with the lemon wedges.

Cubes of at least one-day old bread, speared on cocktail sticks, are the usual accompaniment.

SERVES 8

www.thegreekfood.com

Octopus Cooked In Wine

1 3/4 lb. octopus (thawed)
4 tbs. olive oil
2 large onions sliced
salt and pepper
1 bay leaf
1/4 cup dry white wine

Directions:

Remove head section from octopus. Clean. Wash arms.
Slice the octopus into bite-sized chunks. Cook in olive oil over medium flame about 10 minutes, turning regularly.
Add onions, seasoning and wine. Cover and simmer gently until the octopus is tender, about 15 minutes.

Serves 4

Sicilian grilled baby octopus

MAKES 4 SERVINGS

INGREDIENTS:

2½ pounds cleaned and frozen baby octopus
2 cups full-bodied red wine, such as
Pinot Noir or Cabernet Sauvignon
1 small onion, sliced
1 teaspoon black peppercorns
teaspoon whole cloves
1 bay leaf
1 cup Sicilian Citrus Marinade
¾cup pitted and coarsely chopped Sicilian or
Cerignola green olives
3 ounces baby arugula leaves
1 tablespoon chopped fresh mint
Coarse sea salt and freshly ground black pepper

DIRECTIONS:

Rinse the octopus, and then put in a soup pot with
the wine and enough water to cover. Add the onion,
peppercorns, cloves, and bay leaf. Bring to a boil
over high heat, and then reduce the heat to
medium-low, cover, and simmer gently until the
octopus is tender enough for a knife to enter

easily, 45 minutes to 1 hour. Drain the octopus and discard the liq-uid or strain and reserve for seafood stock or risotto. When the octopus is cool enough to handle, cut the tentacles away at the head.

Combine the octopus and marinade in a 1-gallon zipper-lock bag. Press out the air, seal the bag, and refrigerate for 2 to 3 hours. Light a grill for direct medium-high heat, about 450$\frac{1}{4}$F .

Remove the octopus from the marinade, pat dry, and let stand at room temperature for 20 minutes. Strain the marinade into a saucepan and bring to a simmer over medium heat. Add the olives and remove from the heat.

Brush the grill grate and coat with oil. Grill the octopus directly over the heat until nicely grill-marked, 3 to 4 minutes per side, pressing gently on the octopus to get a good sear. Arrange the arugula on a platter or plates and top with the octopus. Spoon some of the warm sauce, including a good amount of olives, on each serving. Sprinkle with the mint, salt, and black pepper.

SCALLOPS

Seafood Pot Pie

- 1/2 cup dry white wine
- 1 pound sea scallops, cut in half if very large
- 1 large baking potato, peeled and cut into 1/2 inch dice
- 3 tablespoons butter, softened
- 1/2 cup peeled and minced tart apple
- 1 large carrot, minced
- 1 celery rib, minced
- 1 large onions, minced
- 1 garlic clove, minced
- 1 1/2 cups chicken broth
- 1/4 cup heavy cream
- 2 tablespoons all-purpose flour
- 3/4 teaspoon salt
- 1/2 teaspoon freshly ground white pepper
  Pinch of cayenne pepper
- 1 pound medium shrimp, shelled and deveined
- 1 cup corn kernels
- 1 small jar (3 1/2 ounces) pimiento strips
- 2 tablespoons minced parsley
- Flaky Pastry

In a medium nonreactive saucepan, bring the wine to a boil over high heat. Add the scallops and cook until just opaque throughout, about 1 minute. Drain the scallops, reserving the liquid. In another medium saucepan of boiling salted water, cook the potato until just tender, 6 to 8 minutes; drain and set aside.

Preheat the oven to 425F. In a large saucepan, melt 2 tablespoons of the butter over moderately high heat. Add the apple, carrot, celery and onion and cook until the mixture softens and starts to brown, about 6 minutes. Add the garlic and cook for 1 minute longer. Pour in the chicken stock and increase the heat to high. Boil until most of the liquid has evaporated, about 5 minutes.

Transfer the apple-vegetable mixture to a food processor. Puree until smooth. Return to the saucepan and stir in the reserved scallop liquid and the heavy cream.

In a small bowl, blend the flour into the remaining 1 tablespoon of butter to form a paste. Bring the scallop cream to a simmer over moderate heat. Gradually whisk in the butter paste. Bring to a boil, whisking until

Baked Scallops with Garlic Sauce

- 1 1/2 pounds bay scallops, cut in halves
- 3 cloves garlic, mashed
- 1/4 cup (1/2 stick) margarine, melted
- 10 firm white mushrooms, sliced
- Light dash of onion salt
- Dash of freshly grated pepper
- 1/3 cup seasoned bread crumbs
- 1 teaspoon finely minced fresh parsley

Wipe scallops with damp paper towel. Mash garlic cloves and add to margarine; stir well to blend. Keep warm. Pour a little of the melted garlic sauce into the bottom of a baking dish; add the mushrooms and season. Place the scallops on top of the mushrooms. Reserve 1 tablespoon garlic sauce and drizzle the rest on scallops. Sprinkle with bread crumbs, parsley and reserved garlic sauce. Bake in preheated 375 degrees F oven until the top is nicely browned and bubbly hot.

Scallops Provencal

- 2 teaspoons olive oil
- 1 pound sea scallops
- 1/2 cup thinly sliced onion, separated into rings 1 garlic clove, minced
- 1 cup diced regular or plum tomatoes
- 1/4 cup chopped ripe olives
- 1 tablespoon dried basil
- 1/4 teaspoon dried thyme
- 1/8 teaspoon salt
- 1/8 teaspoon freshly ground pepper

Heat olive oil in a large nonstick skillet over medium-high heat. Add scallops, and sauté 4 minutes or until done. Remove scallops from skillet with a slotted spoon; set aside, and keep warm. Add onion rings and garlic to skillet, and sauté for 1-2 minutes. Add tomato and remaining ingredients and sauté 2 minutes or until tender.

Spoon sauce over scallops

Scallops With White Butter Sauce

- 750g (1=lb) scallops 1= cups white wine 90g(3ozs) snow peas or thinly sliced green beans a few chives to garnish salt and freshly ground pepper a little lemon juice
- 1 Tbs chopped green onion 125g(4ozs) butter cut in pieces

Remove any beards from the scallops then wash. Carefully remove the roes and lay on paper towels to dry. Season with salt and pepper. Poach the scallops and roes in wine and lemon juice for approx. 2 Minutes. Remove and keep warm. String snow peas drop into boiling salted water for 1 min., drain, do the same with beans if using. Add the green onion to the poaching liquid and reduce to about 1/2 cup. Over a gentle heat, add butter a little at a time, whisking it in to make a sauce (the consistency of pouring cream).

Serve with crusty bread to mop up the lovely sauce.

HADDOCK

Haddock with Herbed Butter over Caramelized Onions and Tomatoes

Makes 4 servings

Herbed Butter:

- 1 cup (2 sticks) unsalted butter, softened
- ½ cup loosely packed basil
- ½ cup loosely packed parsley
- ½ shallot
- 1 small clove garlic
- ½ teaspoon salt
- 1/8-teaspoon pepper
- Caramelized Onions:
- 1-tablespoon butter
- 2 large onions, sliced
- ½ teaspoon salt
- ¼ teaspoon freshly ground black pepper
- 2 tablespoons fresh thyme leaves, or 1 teaspoon dried
- 2 pounds haddock
- 3 tomatoes, sliced

- Make the herbed butter by processing the softened butter, basil, parsley, shallot, garlic, salt and pepper together.
- Turn the butter on to a piece of plastic wrap and form the butter into a log. Wrap it in the plastic wrap and chill or freeze. Heat the butter and oil in a medium skillet over medium-low heat.
- Add the onions and cook until they begin to soften, stirring occasionally, about 15 minutes.
- Add the salt and pepper; raise heat slightly, and cook until golden brown, stirring occasionally, 30 to 35 minutes. Stir in the thyme.
- Preheat oven to 375°. Oil a 9 x 13-inch pan.
- Spread the onions in the bottom of the pan, and then place the haddock on the onions.
- Cover the haddock with the sliced tomatoes.
- Bake until the haddock is still a tiny bit opaque in the middle (about 20 minutes). It will keep cooking when you remove it from the oven.
- Slice the herbed butter into $\frac{1}{4}$-inch medallions and place them on top of the tomatoes and serve.

Cajun Spiced Haddock

- 1 Haddock Fillet
- Plain Flour
- 1 tsp. Cajun Spice
- 75g Pineapple diced
- 1 Spring Onion
- 10g Red Onion
- 10g Red Pepper
- 10g Olive Oil

1. For the salsa dice the pineapple roughly into 1cm cubes, finely dice red onion, 1 spring onion, and roasted and skinned red pepper. Add the oil and red wine vinegar and leave in a covered bowl at room temperature for 1 hour.

2. Mix the flour with the Cajun spice and coat the seasoned haddock fillet.

3. Pan Fry the haddock and serve topped with the salsa.

Haddock, Leek & Potato Chowder

- 1/4 Haddock Fillet
- 25g Sliced Leek
- 25g Herby Diced
- Potato
- 15g Diced Onion
- 250ml Cream
- 100ml Fish Stock
- Chopped Parsley

1. Pan Fry the washed and chopped leek.

2. When the leek has softened add the potato and onion.

3. Once the vegetables are warm add the cream and stock and bring to the boil. Turn down to a simmer and add the chopped haddock.

4. Simmer for 10 minutes and add chopped parsley as you serve.

Smoked haddock & Tomato Chutney

Ingredients:

- 3 x 175g smoked haddock fillets (un dyed)
- 30 small readymade tartlet cups

Rarebit

- 325g strong Cheddar cheese
- 75ml milk
- 1 egg yolk
- 1 whole egg
- 1/2 tablespoon mustard powder
- 30g plain flour
- 1/2 teaspoon Worcester sauce, Tabasco sauce
- 25g fresh white breadcrumbs
- Seasoning

Tomato Chutney

- 15g root ginger
- 4 red chillies
- 2kg red tomatoes
- 500g apples, peeled and chopped
- 200g sultanas
- 400g chunky chopped shallots
- Salt

- 450g brown sugar
- 570ml malt vinegar
- Season the haddock well and place in the oven with a little olive oil and cook for about 5-6 minutes.
- Grate the cheese and add to the pan with the milk and gently warm in a pan until dissolved, remove from the heat and cool.
- Add the whole egg and yolk, mustard, breadcrumbs and a dash of both Worcester and Tabasco, season and allow cooling.
- Flake the haddock to remove any bones and place the chutney in the bottom of the tarts, top with the flaked fish. Preheat the grill to a high heat and top the haddock with the rarebit and place under the grill until golden brown on top.
- Remove the haddock from the grill and serve at once.

SWORDFISH

Mandarin sesame swordfish

Soy sauce and sesame add unexpected taste and crunch to swordfish in this Asian-style dish.

Serves: 4

1/2 cup fresh orange juice
2 tablespoons soy sauce
2 teaspoons sesame oil
2 teaspoons grated fresh gingerroot
4 (6-ounce) swordfish steaks
1 (11-ounce) can mandarin oranges, drained
1 tablespoon sesame seeds, toasted

In a large resealable plastic storage bag, combine orange juice, soy sauce, sesame oil, and ginger; add fish, seal bag, and marinate in refrigerator for 30 minutes. Remove fish from marinade, reserving marinade.

Preheat grill to medium-high heat.

Place fish on an oiled grill rack. Grill fish 6 to 7 minutes per side, or until it flakes easily with a fork.

Meanwhile, place reserved marinade in a saucepan and bring to a boil over high heat. Let boil until reduced and thickened. Add mandarin oranges and pour over swordfish. Sprinkle with sesame seeds and serve.

Spicy swordfish steaks

- 4 (4 oz) Swordfish steaks
- 1/4 tsp. Cayenne, thyme, and oregano
- 2 Tbsp. Paprika
- 2 Tbsp. Margarine or butter (melted)
- 1/2 tsp. Salt, pepper, onion, and garlic powder

For an appetizer, cut the swordfish steaks into small strips. For a meal, leave swordfish steaks whole. Mix all seasons together. Dip fish in melted butter. Coat both sides with seasoning. Place on grill. Cook approximately 4 minutes; turn, and cook approximately 4 minutes more or until fish is firm and flaky. Makes 4 servings.

SALMON

Salmon with grilled onions

MAKES 8 TO 10 SERVINGS

2 cups hardwood chips, soaked in water
1 large side farmed Norwegian salmon (about 3 pounds), pin bones removed
3 cups Smoking Brine, made with vodka
¾ cup Smoking Rub
1 tablespoon dried dill weed
1 teaspoon onion powder
2 large red onions, cut into -inch-thick rounds
¾ cup extra-virgin olive oil 1 bunch fresh dill
Finely grated zest of 1 lemon 1 garlic clove, minced
Coarse salt and ground black pepper

DIRECTIONS:

Put the salmon in a jumbo (2-gallon) zipper-lock bag. If you only have 1-gallon bags, cut the fish in half and use two bags. Add the brine to the bag(s), press out the air, and seal. Refrigerate for 3 to 4 hours.

Mix all but 1 tablespoon of the rub with the dried dill and onion powder and set aside. Soak the onion slices in ice water. Heat a grill for indirect low heat, about 225iF, with smoke. Drain the wood chips and add them to the grill. Remove the salmon from the brine and pat dry with paper towels. Discard the brine. Coat the fish with 1 tablespoon of the oil and sprinkle the meaty side with the rub that has dried dill in it.

Lift the onions from the ice water and pat dry. Coat with 1 tablespoon of the oil and sprinkle with the remaining 1 tablespoon rub. Set the fish and onions aside to rest for 15 minutes. Brush the grill grate and rub well with oil. Place the salmon, flesh-side down, directly over the heat and grill for 5 minutes until the surface is golden brown. Using a large fish spatula or two regular spatulas, turn the fish skin-side down and position on the grill grate away from the fire. Put the onion slices directly over the fire. Close the grill and cook until the salmon is firm on the outside, but not dry, and resilient in the center, about 25 minutes. When done, moisture will bead through the surface when the fish is gently pressed. It should not fully flake under pressure. Turn the onions once during the cooking time.

Cedar plank salmon

Serves: 6

Cooking Time: 20 min

1 untreated cedar plank (about 14" x 17" x 1/2")
1/2 cup Italian dressing
1/4 cup chopped sun-dried tomatoes
1/4 cup chopped fresh basil

1 (2-pound) salmon fillet (1 inch thick), skin removed

Completely immerse cedar plank in water, placing a weight on top to keep it totally covered. Soak at least 1 hour.

Preheat grill to medium-high heat.

In a small bowl, combine dressing, sun-dried tomatoes, and basil; set aside.

Remove plank from water. Place salmon on plank; place on grill and close lid. Grill 10 minutes then brush salmon with dressing mixture. Close lid and grill 10 more minutes, or until salmon flakes easily with a fork.

Smoked garlic salmon

Serves 4

Ingredients

1 1/2 lbs salmon fillet
salt and pepper to taste 3 garlic cloves, minced
1 sprig fresh dill, chopped 5 slices lemon

Rubbing

5 sprigs fresh dill weed
2 green onions, chopped

Cooking Directions

Prepare smoker to 250° F.

Spray two large pieces of aluminum foil with
cooking spray.

Place salmon fillet on top of one piece of foil.
Sprinkle salmon with salt, pepper, garlic and
chopped dill. Arrange lemon slices on top of fillet
and place a sprig of dill on top of each lemon slice.
Sprinkle fillet with green onions.

Smoke for about 45 minutes.

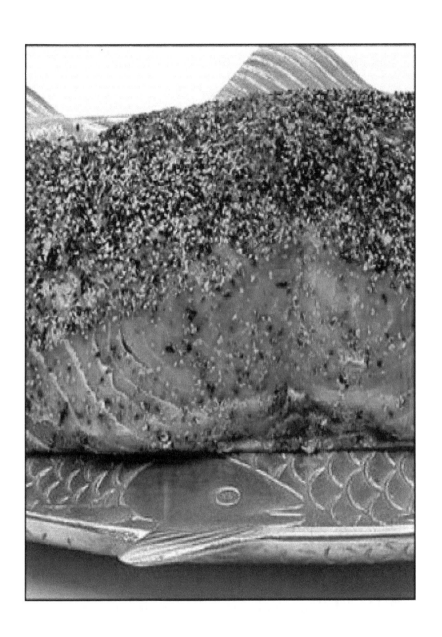

Salmon with tarragon dill cream sauce

THE PREPARATION
Salmon Filets
- 1 1/2 lb. Salmon Filet
- 3/4-1 tsp. Dried Tarragon
- 3/4-1 tsp. Dried Dill Weed
- 1 tbsp. Duck Fat
- Salt and Pepper to Taste

Cream Sauce
- 2 tbsp. Butter
- 1/4 cup Heavy Cream
- 1/2 tsp. Dried Tarragon
- 1/2 tsp. Dried Dill Weed
- Salt and Pepper to Taste

THE EXECUTION
1. Slice the salmon in half to create 2 1/4 lb. filets. Season meat of fish with tarragon, dill weed, and salt and pepper. Turn around and season skin with salt and pepper only.

2. Heat 1 tbsp. duck fat in a ceramic cast iron skillet over medium heat (or any pan that will hold heat well). Once hot, add salmon skin side down.

3. Allow salmon to cook for 4-6 minutes while skin crisps up. Once the skin is crisp, reduce to low heat and flip salmon.

4. Cook salmon until done-ness you want is achieved. Generally about 7-15 minutes over low heat.
Optional: If desired, cook on sides for 20-40 seconds to get darker edges.

5. Remove salmon from the pan and set aside. Add butter and spices to the pan and let brown. Once browned, add cream mix together.

6. Serve with broccoli or asparagus (or your favorite side dish) and be generous with cream sauce. Garnish with a small amount of red pepper flakes.

Blackened Salmon

6 Salmon Fillets, 1/2 - 3/4 inch thick, skinned

2 1/2 cups unsalted butter or margarine

1/2 cup fresh lemon juice

1 1/2 teaspoons cayenne pepper

1 teaspoon salt

2 teaspoons fresh ground black pepper

1 Tablespoon dried thyme

Lemon wedges and Parsley for garnish

Trim off the thin edges of fillets as these would burn. Pat dry and refrigerate until ready to cook. The butter sauce adheres better to cold fillets.

In heavy 3-quart cast-iron frying pan over medium heat, melt butter, add lemon juice, cayenne, salt, black pepper and thyme. Stir to blend; cool to lukewarm.

Place an empty 10-inch cast-iron skillet over high heat until bottom has a definite white haze and begins to smoke slightly. Remove fish from refrigerator; dip 1 fillet in warm butter sauce, coating well. Place fish in hot skillet, taking care that spits and spatters do not burn you. Fish will sear and cook almost immediately. Turn fillet over; blacken other side. Repeat with remaining fillets.

Reserve remaining butter sauce. As fillets are cooked, place them on individual plates; keep warm. Discard accumulated butter sauce in skillet and charred bits between batches. When all fillets have been cooked, wipe skillet clean and place empty skillet back on heat. Add reserved butter sauce; carefully swirl skillet 5 or 6 times to blacken butter. Remove pan from heat; drizzle butter over each fillet. Garnish and serve hot.

Magic baked salmon

(Makes 1 serving)

- 1 salmon fillet
- 2 teaspoons Salmon Magic
- Unsalted butter, melted

Heat oven to 450 F.

Lightly brush the top and sides of the salmon fillet with melted butter. Lightly brush a small sheet pan with melted butter.
Season the top and sides of the salmon fillet with the Salmon Magic. If the fillet is thick, use a little more Salmon Magic. Press the seasoning in gently. Place the fillet on the sheet pan and bake until the top is golden brown, and the fillet is just cooked through. In order to have moist, pink salmon, do not overcook. Serve immediately.
Cook time: 4 to 6 minutes.

Pan-seared salmon with zucchini pesto

INGREDIENTS

Zucchini Pasto

- 3 ripe medium-size tomatoes, cored and quartered
- 2 tablespoons extra-virgin olive oil (preferably Spanish olive oil)
- 1 medium yellow onion, finely chopped
- 1 garlic clove, very finely chopped
- 1 red bell pepper--halved, seeded and chopped into $\frac{1}{4}$-inch pieces
- 2 medium zucchini, ends trimmed and zucchini chopped into $\frac{1}{4}$-inch pieces
- 1 sprig fresh rosemary
- 1 sprig fresh thyme
- 1 teaspoon kosher salt

Salmon
- Four 6- to 8-ounce salmon fillets, pin bones removed
- 1 teaspoon kosher salt
- 1 teaspoon freshly ground black pepper
- 1 tablespoon extra-virgin olive oil (preferably Spanish olive oil)

DIRECTIONS

Make the zucchini pesto: To a blender, add the tomato quarters and purée until smooth. Set aside. In a large skillet set over medium-high heat, add the 2 tablespoons olive oil and the onion. Cook, stirring often, until the onion is translucent, 2 to 3 minutes. Add the garlic and stir until fragrant, about 30 seconds. Reduce the heat to medium-low and add the red bell pepper, stirring occasionally, until it begins to soften, about 10 minutes. Stir in the zucchini and cook until it begins to soften, about 8 minutes. Add the blended tomatoes and simmer on low heat until the pesto looks thick and has reduced by half, about 35 minutes. Add the rosemary and thyme sprigs and simmer for 5 minutes. Turn off the heat and discard the rosemary and thyme. Season with the 1 teaspoon of salt.

Cook the salmon: Use paper towels to pat both sides of each salmon fillet dry. Season the fillets with the 1 teaspoon of salt and the black pepper. In a large skillet set over high heat, add the 1 tablespoon of olive oil. Once the oil begins to shimmer, add 2 of the salmon fillets, skin side down. Cook the salmon without moving the fillets until the skin is browned, about 4 minutes. Use a fish spatula to gently flip each fillet over, and cook until the center of the fillets are semi-firm, about

3 minutes more. Transfer to a plate and repeat with the remaining 2 salmon fillets. Serve with the zucchini pesto.

Poached Salmon in Tomato Garlic Broth

Serves 4

- 8 cloves garlic
- shallots
- teaspoons extra virgin olive oil
- 5 ripe tomatoes
- 1 1/2 cups dry white wine
- 1 cup water
- 8 sprigs of thyme 1/4 teaspoon sea salt
- 1/4 teaspoon fresh black pepper
- 4 Copper River Sockeye Salmon fillets white truffle oil (optional)

Peel and roughly chop garlic cloves and shallots. In a large braising dish or sauté pan with a lid, place the olive oil, garlic, and shallots. Sweat over medium-low heat until soft, about 3 minutes.

Place the tomatoes, wine, water, thyme, salt, and pepper in the pan and bring to a boil. Once boiling, reduce heat to a simmer and cover. Simmer for 25 minutes until the tomatoes have burst releasing their juices. With a wooden spoon or spatula, crush the tomatoes into a pulp. Simmer uncovered for another 5 minutes until the broth has reduced a little.

While the broth is still simmering, place the salmon in the broth. Cover and poach for 5 to 6 minutes only until the fish easily flakes. Place the fish on a plate and set aside. Place a strainer into a large bowl and pour the remaining broth into the strainer. Strain the broth discarding the solids that remain. Taste the broth and add salt and pepper if needed.

Simple butter mashed potatoes or even roasted potatoes are a good side with this meal. To plate, I place mashed potatoes in a large bowl or a deep plate. Then top with sauteed asparagus and the poached salmon. Pour the strained broth around the salmon. Add a drizzle of white truffle oil if desired. Serve.

Prosciutto/Salmon Wraps

- 2 avocados, seeded and peeled
- 8 slices each prosciutto and smoked salmon
  Fresh lemon or lime
- Cut each avocado into 8 slices. Diagonally wrap each with a prosciutto or salmon slice. Arrange wraps on serving platter, garnish with lemon or lime and serve.

Salmon Croquettes

- 15 oz. Can of red or pink salmon, drained
- 1 Small onion, finely chopped
- 1 Teaspoon Fresh lemon juice
- 1 Egg, lightly beaten
- 12-15 Saltine crackers, crushed
- $\frac{1}{4}$ Teaspoon Ground pepper
- 2 Teaspoon Fresh parsley, chopped (optional)
- $\frac{1}{4}$ Cup Canola oil

Mash drained salmon in a bowl. Add chopped onion, lemon juice, egg, pepper and, if desired, parsley. Mix gently. Shape into six croquettes (patties).

Crush the saltines between two sheets of waxed paper with a rolling pin. Set each croquette into the crumbs, pressing gently to make sure crumbs adhere, turning to coat both sides.

Heat oil in skillet over medium heat. Fry croquettes on one side until golden brown, then gently turn and fry other side. Serves 4 to 6, depending upon appetites.

Salmon Pate

- 1 cup salmon, flaked
- 1 pkg. (8 oz.) cream cheese, room temperature
- 1 tablespoon fresh lemon juice
- 1 teaspoon prepared horseradish
- 1 teaspoon onion, grated
- 1/4 teaspoon salt
- 1/8 teaspoon pepper
- 1/8 teaspoon liquid smoke

Garnish:
- almond slices
- parsley
- Olives
- Celery

Mix Salmon with all of the other ingredients. Press into a fish shaped mold or shape by hand as such. Garnish fish with almond slices to resemble scales. Slice green olive for eye and thin strips of celery for tail. Garnish top with parsley. Chill at least 1 hour before serving.

Spice-Rubbed Salmon with Sautéed Greens

- 4 4-ounce salmon fillets*
- 1 tablespoon fennel seeds
- 1 teaspoon coriander seeds
- 1 tablespoon lemon juice
- 2 tablespoons olive oil
- salt and pepper, to taste
- lemon or lime slices (optional)

*We used salmon steaks, which we cut in half and deboned. You can choose to keep the skin off or remove it before cooking.

Rinse the salmon fillets and trim/debone if necessary. Place in a large bowl.

Using a spice grinder or mortar and pestle, coarsely grind the coriander and fennel seeds together. Add the seeds, salt and pepper, lemon juice and oil to the fish and rub the spices into each side of the salmon fillets. Let sit for a few minutes as you turn your oven's broiler to high. Place the fish on a lined baking sheet, topping with the lemon or lime slices if desired. Broil for 6 minutes, turning halfway.

For the greens:

- 2 tablespoons olive oil
- 1 clove garlic, sliced
- 5 ounces mixed greens, such as spinach, chard and dandelion (we used a Satur Farms stir-fry blend), trimmed and rinsed
- 1 teaspoon crushed red pepper
- salt and pepper, to taste

Heat the oil on medium in a large skillet. Add the garlic and saute until slightly browned. Add the greens, crushed red pepper, salt and pepper, and saute until the greens are wilted, about 5 minutes.

Smoked Salmon and Scrambled Eggs

Serves: 2

Ingredients

8 fresh eggs
Knob of butter
150g pack of smoked salmon
Salt and pepper
2 slices Sourdough bread

Method

Pre-heat griddle pan. Heat your non-stick pan gently and add a knob of the butter. And add your beaten eggs. Gently cook and stir. Continue to cook for a couple of minutes, whilst still just underdone. Griddle the bread until nicely charred on each side. When the eggs thicken, season with salt and pepper and pile the eggs over the toast. Top with smoked salmon slices.

Serve with a good wedge of lemon and freshly ground black pepper.

Stovetop Smoked Salmon with Dill-Lemon Aioli

smoking chips
1-1/2 lb. fresh boneless salmon filet, about 1-inch thick
juice of 1/2 lime
2 Tbsp. white wine
1 Tbsp. mayonnaise
1/2 tsp. kosher salt
1/2 tsp. onion powder
1/2 tsp. garlic powder
1/2 tsp. lemon pepper
1/2 tsp. dried oregano
1/2 tsp. dried dill weed
1/4 tsp. paprika

Sprinkle smoking chips over the bottom of the smoker. Place drip pan over chips. (Line drip pan with foil for easier clean-up, but make sure the foil is pressed tightly to the pan so you don't disrupt the air-flow of the smoke.) Brush wire grill rack with vegetable oil and place in drip pan. Place fish on rack.

Squeeze lime over salmon. Drizzle with wine. Combine remaining ingredients, brush mixture onto top of fish.

Position smoker over one stovetop burner as evenly as possible. Heat smoker on medium-high and offset lid so it is not tightly closed. When wisps of smoke begin to come through the opening, re-position the lid so it is tightly closed.

Cook 15 to 25 min., depending on the thickness of the fish. The fish should just barely give to the touch, like a medium-cooked steak. Let rest 5 min. before serving with aioli.

Dill-Lemon Aioli

2 egg yolks
1/2 tsp. lemon zest
1/4 cup lemon juice
3 garlic cloves, minced
1-1/2 tsp. chopped fresh parsley
1 tsp. kosher salt
3/4 tsp. dried dill weed
1/4 tsp. Worcestershire sauce
1/8 tsp. cayenne pepper
3/4 cup olive oil

Place all ingredients, except oil, in a blender. Pulse to combine.

With blender running, very slowly drizzle in olive oil, little by little, until an emulsion forms (the mixture will thicken and become a creamy, white color).

Refrigerate 1 hour prior to serving to allow flavors to combine.

Soy-Ginger Marinated Salmon

4 salmon fillets or steaks (allow about 6 oz. per person)
Marinade (see following recipe)
Lemon wedges, optional

Marinade:

1 cup sake (Japanese rice wine)
1/2 cup natural soy sauce or tamari (preferably reduced sodium)
1 tbsp. fresh grated ginger

2 cloves fresh garlic, pressed
1 tablespoon dark brown sugar

Make the marinade by whisking the marinade ingredients together in a small bowl.

Rinse the salmon fillets under cold water, and place in a glass or ceramic dish. Pour the marinade over the fish. Cover the dish and allow the fish to marinate in the refrigerator for several hours (about one to three hours). At least once or twice during this time, check the fish and spoon the marinade over any exposed parts of the fillets.

Fire the grill, or preheat the broiler to high heat.

Drain the fish and place on foil on grill or rack in the oven. Cook until desired doneness, (fish flakes easily and is opaque) but be careful not to overcook.

Serve immediately, with lemon wedges as garnish if you like. For a complete, satisfying meal, add rice and a salad or steamed vegetables.

Makes four servings.

Sweet Salmon with Ginger and Scallions

2 (1-inch thick) salmon filets

2 scallions, cut into 2-inch long strips

1/4 cup ginger, cut into 1/4-inch thick chunks

1 1/2 tablespoons olive oil

1/4 cup white wine, rice wine or sweet sake

1/2 cup water

1 tablespoon soy sauce

1 teaspoon granulated sugar

Salt and pepper

Sesame oil (optional)

Heat oil in pan on high heat. Salt and pepper both sides of the salmon filets.

Place filets in pan skin-side down and do not disturb. Cook on high for 40 sec. Turn heat down to medium-high and continue to cook for 3 minutes.

Turn filets over and cook for another 2 minutes. Remove filets from pan and set aside on a plate.

Turn heat back up to high and add ginger and scallions. Cook until slightly tender (about 1 minute). Add wine and deglaze pan. Add soy sauce, water, and sugar. Bring to a boil, then reduce heat to simmer.

Place salmon filets carefully back into pan and simmer until salmon is cooked through (about 2 minutes). Drizzle with a few drops of sesame oil if desired.

Serves 2 to 3.

Butter Barbecued Salmon

- 6--8 lb whole salmon, cleaned
- salt & pepper, to taste
- 2 cups chopped mushrooms
- 1 cup chopped green onions
- 2 tbs minced parsley
- 1/2 cup grated Parmesan cheese Grated peel and juice of 1 lemon
- 1/2 cup (1 stick) butter or margarine, melted 4-5 lemon slices
- sauces: butter, chili-cheese, or tartar

Remove head from salmon, if desired. Place salmon on double thickness of wide foil, making sure foil is three to four inches longer than fish at each end. Sprinkle fish inside and out with salt and pepper to taste. Combine mushrooms, onion, parsley, cheese, lemon peel, and juice.

Spoon mixture into fish cavity. Pour butter over fish and top with lemon slices. Cover with another thickness of foil and carefully seal all sides completely. Place on grill four to six inches from glowing coals. Turn after 30 minutes and cook 20 to 30 minutes longer. If cooking on smoke-type grill, open foil during last ten minutes and close grill cover so smoke flavor penetrates fish. Serve with choice of sauces. Makes 10 to 12 servings.

Butter Sauce

- 1/2 cup butter or margarine
- 1 cup sour cream
- 1/4 tsp seasoned or onion salt
- 1 tsp chopped chives

Melt butter in small saucepan over low heat.

Stir in sour cream, seasoned salt, and chives.

Warm, but do not boil.

Curried Salmon-Rice Loaf

1 can (17 1/2 ounce) salmon

1/3 cup chopped green onions

2 tsp curry powder

1 tbs lemon juice

1 tbs cider vinegar

1 tbs chopped or powdered garlic

3 cups cooked rice

Lettuce

Flake salmon. Remove skin and bones. Add salmon, green onions, curry powder, lemon juice, cider vinegar, and garlic to rice. Mix well. Pack into plastic-lined loaf pan and chill several hours in refrigerator. When ready to serve, unmold onto lettuce--lined platter. Makes 4 servings.

Salmon-Broccoli Loaf with Dill and Capers

1 c loosely packed parseley sprigs, washed & patted dry on paper towels

6 slices firm-textured white bread

2 c 1/2 inch cubes of broccoli stems (the amt you'll get from one large bunch of broccoli. Amount can be variable.)

1 medium yellow onion, cut into slim wedges

1 3/4 pounds cooked or canned boned salmon (remove all dark skin)

1/3 c drained caperss (use the small capers)

2/3 c light cream

4 eggs

2 TBS snipped fresh dill or 3/4 tsp dill weed Finely grated rind of 1/2 lemon 1/8 tsp freshly ground black pepper

In food processor fitted with metal chopping blade, mince paresely fine, using 5-6 on-offs of the motor; empty into a large mixing bowl. Now crumb the bread 2 slices at a time, with two or three 5- or 6 churning of the motor; add to bowl. Dump all the broccoli stems into processor; mince very fine with about three 5-second bursts; add to bowl.

Processor-mince the onion -- 3 o4 4 bursts will do it -- add to the bowl.

Flake the salmon in three batches -- 2 on-offs will be enough. Add to the mixing bowl along with all remaining ingredients. Mix v thoroughly, pack mixture firmly into a well-buttered 9x5x3 inch loaf pan and bake in a slow oven (300 degrees F.) for about 1 hour and 40 minutes, or until loaf begins to pull from sides of pan and is firm to the touch. Remove loaf from oven and let it stand upright in its pan on a wire rack for 30 minutes. Carefully loosen the loaf all around w a thin-bladed spatula, then invert gently onto a large serving platter.

Salmon in Vodka Cream Sauce with Green Peppercorns

8 tablespoons butter
1 onion, thinly sliced
1 pound spinach
6 6 ounce salmon fliets
salt and freshly ground pepper
3 tablespoons olive oil
1 1/2 cups whipping cream
1/2 cup vodka
2 tablespoons green peppercorns in water, drained
and crushed
3 tablespoons fresh lime juice
1/4 cup snipped fresh chives

Preheat oven to 350F. Combine 4 tablespoons
butter and onion in large Dutch oven. Cover and
bake until onion is golden brown, stirring
occasionally, about 45 minutes.

Stir spinach into onion and bake until just wilted,
about 3 minutes.
Remove from oven; keep warm.

Season salmon with salt and pepper. Heat oil in heavy large skillet over high heat. Add salmon in batches and cook about 3 minutes per side for medium. Transfer to platter. Tent with foil to keep warm. Pour off excess oil from skillet. Add cream and vodka and boil until slightly thickened, about 4 minutes. Add green peppercorns and remaining 4 tablespoons butter and stir until butter is just melted. Mix in lime juice, season with salt and pepper.

Divide spinach and onion mixture among plates. Top each with salmon fillet. Spoon sauce over. Sprinkle with snipped fresh chives.

Salmon with Basil Cream Sauce

Ingredients:

- 2 lbs. salmon fillets
- 1 1/2 T unsalted butter
- 3 shallots, peeled and minced
- 1 clove garlic, peeled and minced
- 1 1/2 cup chopped fresh basil
- 1/4 cup chopped fresh parsley
- 3/4 cup dry white wine
- 1/3 cup light cream
- 1T freshly squeezed lemon juice
- 1/4 t freshly ground white pepper
- 1/4 t salt, or to taste

Cut the salmon into 6 equal serving pieces, wash and pat dry on paper towels. Melt the butter in a large skillet over medium-high heat. Sear the salmon on each side for about 2 to

3 minutes, keeping the center slightly rare since the fish will continue to cook after it is taken from the pan. Remove the fish from the pan with a slotted spatula and keep warm. Reduce the heat to low and add the shallots and garlic to the pan. Sauté, stirring frequently, for 5 minutes

Add the basil, parsley, wine, cream, lemon juice, pepper and salt to the pan and cook over medium heat, stirring frequently, until the mixture is reduced by half. Taste for seasoning, adding pepper and salt as needed.

To serve, reheat the fish slightly in the sauce and then serve the sauce around the salmon fillets.

NOTE: The fish can be prepared up to three hours in advance. Reheat the fish in the sauce over low heat, uncovered, for 10 minutes.

Salmon with Cumin-Coriander Crema & Chipotle Salsa

Rinse and dry each salmon fillet. It is not necessary to remove the skin from the fillets. Check for pinbones by running your fingertips over the flesh side of the fillet. Use pliers or tweezers to remove any bones.

In a small bowl stir together the oregano, basil, and parsley. Pat the herbs onto the flesh side of each fillet, covering well. Refrigerate until ready to cook.

To prepare the crema, combine the cumin and coriander seeds in a small, dry saute pan over medium heat. Roast the seeds, shaking the pan frequently, until the aromas are released, about 2 minutes. Remove from the heat and let cool. Place the spices in a spice mill or coffee grinder and grind to pulverize the seeds. Alternatively, pulverize in a mortar using a pestle.

In a small bowl, combine the ground seeds with all the remaining crema ingredients. Let sit for 30 minutes so the flavors can develop and blend. Pour through a fine-mesh strainer into a bowl to remove the cilantro leaves. You will have about 1 cup. (The crema will keep for up to 1 week in the refrigerator.)

To prepare the salsa, place all the ingredients, except the olive oil, in a food processor fitted with the metal blade or in a blender. Blend thoroughly. With the motor running, slowly pour in the olive oil in a thin, steady stream, continuing to process until a mayonnaiselike sauce is achieved. Transfer to a bowl, cover, and refrigerate until serving. You will have about 1 1/4 cups. (The salsa will keep for up to 2 days in the refrigerator.)

About 15 minutes before serving, place a saute' pan large enough to hold the salmon, with room to spare, over medium heat. Add the olive oil. When the oil is just smoking, put the fillets in the pan, herb sides down. Cook

4 to 5 minutes, then turn and cook on the second side until done, 4 to 5 minutes longer. Cooking times vary according to taste and the thickness of the fillet. At Cafe Pasqual's fish is considered done when the middle is still moist and a bit darker than the surrounding light pink flesh. To serve, spoon the crema onto individual plates, dividing it equally among them. Place 1 salmon fillet on each plate, herbed sides up, to cover half the crema.

Drizzle the salsa decoratively onto the fillet and then onto the visible half of the crema.

Spicy Salmon and Eggplant

- 3 fresh salmon steaks
- eggplant
- limes
- lemons
- 1/8 cup olive oil
- 1 tsp. Greek or Italian seasoning 1/8 tsp. hot red pepper flakes Fresh ground black pepper

Remove stem and end of eggplant and slice on a diagonal, cutting slices approximately 1/4-inch thick.

Place salmon steaks and eggplant slices in a large, flat Tupperware container. Cut lemons and limes in half and remove juice.

Pour juice into a separate bowl. Stir in olive oil, seasoning, pepper flakes and ground pepper. Pour over steaks and eggplant. Cover and marinate in refrigerator for 1 to 1-1/2 hours. Turn steaks over and rearrange eggplant for even marinating, once during process. Place steaks on a hot grill and cook on both sides until done. Add eggplant slices to grill when fish is half cooked. Grill eggplant slices on both sides. Remove.

Serve fish and vegetables with rice.

Poached Salmon/Sautéed Tuna

I poach small salmon filets, approximately 6 ounces, by putting about a half inch of water in a small, 5-6 inch fry pan, covering it, heating the water to simmer, then putting in the filet covered for four minutes.

That's it and of course, you can add whatever seasoning you like to the salmon or to the water. I apologize for being so basic, but for years I was afraid to try poaching even though

I adore poached salmon, so I'm telling you exactly how to do it and how easy it is. The four minutes leaves the center uncooked and very juicy. If there's skin, it usually sticks to the pan, and if you run hot water over it as soon as you remove the salmon, it'll wash/scrape right off.

I've taken to letting the filet cool off a bit and cutting it into inch and a half wide pieces and adding to a salad including lettuce (any kind) good tomato, nice ripe avocado, red onion, croutons, and any tasty dressing.

Citrus Salmon

Perparation time: 10 minutes

Cooking Time: 7-10 minutes

- 1 lb (500g) salmon fillets
- Salt and pepper
- 1 tbsp cornstarch
- 1 tbsp water
- 2 tbsp undiluted frozen orange juice concentrate
- 1 tbsp lemon juice
- 1/4 cup brown sugar

Garnish (optional)
- 1 sliced orange
- parsley

Sprinkle both sides of the salmon fillet with salt and pepper. Mix the corn-starch and water in a small bowl to form a paste. Add the orange juice concentrate, lemon juice and brown sugar. Stir mixture well until all the ingredients are dissolved. Set aside.

Pour half of the sauce into the bottom of a microwaveable dish. Place the salmon fillet in the dish on top of sauce. Pour the remaining sauce over the salmon. Cover the dish with plastic wrap. Vent to allow steam to escape.

Microwave on high for 7-10 minutes (depending on microwave)

Remove from microwave and remove plastic wrap. Place the fillet on a plate.

Stir remaining sauce and pour over the fillet and garnish if desired.

Grilled Salmon

I do this with whole salmon, any type, and I leave the skin on as it lifts right off after cooking. Place the salmon on a piece of foil large enough to completely wrap it. Fill the inside of the salmon with a mixture of chopped onion, celery, carrots, garlic and green peppers. Add 2 or 3 slices of lemon and several pats of butter. Salt and pepper to taste if desired, I usually don't tho. Seal the foil and cook on a grill or in an oven. The cooking time depends on the size/amount of fish, it seems that when you can really smell the salmon thru the foil, it is usually done. I know this is not the best method for determining doneness, but it usually works for me.

I do open the foil and test the fish for flakeyness. The stuffing usually absorbs a lot of fat/oil from the fish and is not, in my opinion, all that good, but it adds great flavor to the fish.

Here's a wonderful salmon recipe which I have shamelessly stolen from Delia Smith's summer collection (a fantastic book). I made this recently and it got rave reviews.

Thai salmon parcels

(serves 2)

2 4-5oz salmon fillets
4 sheets filo pastry
1 oz butter   zest & juice 1 lime
1 tsp grated ginger 1 clove garlic   (pressed)
1 spring onion (finely chopped)
1 Tbsp fresh coriander (finely   chopped)

salt & pepper
Mix together lime zest and juice, garlic, spring
onion, ginger and coriander.

Melt butter. Lay out 1 sheet of filo, and brush with
butter. Lay second sheet on top, brush with more
butter. Lay a salmon fillet about 2-3 inches from
short side of pastry, season to taste and put half
of lime mixture on top. Fold short end of pastry
over salmon, then fold in the 2 long sides. Fold the
salmon over twice more, and cut off the remaining
pastry. Do the same with the other fillet.

Put the parcels on a well-greased baking sheet, and
just before baking brush with the remaining
butter.Cook at gas mark 5 for 20-25 Minutes, until
brown and crispy.

Smoked Salmon Dip

Here's what you need:
Light cream cheese-1 package (8 oz.)
Lemon juice-3 Tbsp
 Low-fat milk-3 Tbsp
Smoked Alaska salmon-1 package (8 to 12 oz.)
Thinly sliced green onions-1/4 cup Crackers or
French bread slices-as needed

Here's what you do:
Mix cream cheese with lemon juice and milk until
light and fluffy. Stir in salmon and green onions until
thoroughly combined.

Put it together!
Spread on crackers or French bread slices.

Nutrients per serving: 386 calories, 16g total fat, 6g
saturated fat, 144mg cholesterol, 51g protein, 7g
carbohydrate, 2g fiber, 215mg sodium, 165mg
calcium and 2g omega-3 fatty acids.

Wild Salmon, Chive & Cheddar Grills

Here's what you need:

Canned sockeye (red) or 1 tall (14.75 oz.)
pink wild salmon-7.5 oz. cans
Low fat soft cheese with garlic and herbs-4 oz.
Cheddar cheese, grated-2 oz.
Chopped chives-1 Tbsp
Sourdough or mixed seed bread-4 thick slices

Here's what you do:
Drain the canned salmon. Break the salmon into
chunks.
Add the soft cheese and about two-thirds of the
Cheddar to the salmon. Stir together with the
chives.

Put it together!
Spread the salmon mixture over the slices of bread.
Sprinkle the left over Cheddar over the top, then
place in the toaster oven until melted and bubbling.
Serve at once.

Nutrients per serving: 453 calories, 19g total fat, 9g
saturated fat, 108mg cholesterol, 38g protein, 30g
carbohydrate, 1g fiber, 899mg sodium, 159mg
calcium and 1.5g omega-3 fatty acids.

Salmon Burgers

Here's what you need:
Canned sockeye (red) or pink salmon-1 tall (14.75 oz.)
or 2 short (7.5 oz.) cans
Egg-1 large
Onion, diced (cut into small pieces)-1/2 cup
Salt and pepper to taste
Bread crumbs or crushed crackers-1/2 cup

Here's what you do:
Drain salmon thoroughly. In bowl, flake salmon with
fork. Add egg, onion, salt and pepper and bread
crumbs. Blend thoroughly until mixture is almost
smooth.
Divide equally and form mixture into four patties.
Preheat broiler/oven or grill to medium-high heat.
Place patties on spray-coated broiling pan or well-
oiled grill. Cook about 4 to 5 minutes per side.

Put it together!
Add your favorite fixin's like cheese, tomatoes,
onions or pickles.
Serve on buns or rolls.

Nutrients per serving: 244 calories, 8g total fat,
1.5g saturated fat, 110mg cholesterol, 31g protein,

11g carbohydrate, 1g fiber, 520mg sodium, 69mg calcium and 1.5g omega-3 fatty acids.

Teriyaki Salmon Wrap

HERE'S WHAT YOU DO:

In a large bowl, combine the salmon (if using canned, drain first), cream cheese, teriyaki sauce, and pepper, and stir thoroughly to combine.

In a microwave on a paper towel, warm the tortillas for about 10 seconds each.

Place the warm tortillas on individual plates and evenly spread 1/4 cup of rice in the middle of each. Spread 1/4 cup of the salmon mixture on top of the rice, then top each wrap with lettuce and any sliced vegetables.

Putting it together
Tightly roll each tortilla around the filling from bottom to top, overlapping one end, burrito style. Slice the wraps in half if desired and serve.

Nutrients per serving: 517 calories, 16g total fat, 6g saturated fat, 100mg cholesterol, 44g protein, 52g carbohydrate, 3g fiber, 938mg sodium, 67mg calcium and 1.8g omega-3 fatty acids.

Salmon with tarragon dill cream sauce

THE PREPARATION
Salmon Filets
- 1 1/2 lb. Salmon Filet
- 3/4-1 tsp. Dried Tarragon
- 3/4-1 tsp. Dried Dill Weed
- 1 tbsp. Duck Fat
- Salt and Pepper to Taste

Cream Sauce
- 2 tbsp. Butter
- 1/4 cup Heavy Cream
- 1/2 tsp. Dried Tarragon
- 1/2 tsp. Dried Dill Weed
- Salt and Pepper to Taste

THE EXECUTION
1. Slice the salmon in half to create 2 1/4 lb. filets.
Season meat of fish with
tarragon, dill weed, and salt and pepper. Turn
around and season skin with
salt and pepper only.
2. Heat 1 tbsp. duck fat in a ceramic cast iron
skillet over medium heat (or any
pan that will hold heat well). Once hot, add salmon
skin side down.

3. Allow salmon to cook for 4-6 minutes while skin crisps up. Once the skin is

crisp, reduce to low heat and flip salmon.

4. Cook salmon until done-ness you want is achieved. Generally about 7-15

minutes over low heat.

Optional: If desired, cook on sides for 20-40 seconds to get darker edges.

5. Remove salmon from the pan and set aside. Add butter and spices to the

pan and let brown. Once browned, add cream mix together.

6. Serve with broccoli or asparagus (or your favorite side dish) and be gen-

erous with cream sauce. Garnish with a small amount of red pepper flakes.

This makes 2 total servings of Salmon with Tarragon Dill Cream Sauce.

Each serving comes out to be 469 Calories, 40g Fats, 1.5g Net Carbs, and 22.5g Protein.

SEAFOOD RECIPE COOKBOOK

+50 Fresh & Delicious Recipes to Maintain a Healthy Weight

Ally Rogers

Disclaimer

SHRIMP 158

Spicy grilled shrimp.............................159

Grilled herbed shrimp 162

Shrimp en brochette.............................165

Shrimp packets.....................................168

Basil shrimp 169

Grilled bacon-wrapped shrimp.............. 171

Alabama Shrimp Bake...........................175

Almost Shrimp Paesano 178

Bean & Shrimp Risotto......................... 181

Beer-Broiled Shrimp 184

Boiled Gulf Shrimp...............................185

Rémoulade Sauce...187

California Scampi 190

Champagne Shrimp And Pasta........................192

Coconut Shrimp with Jalapeño Jelly 195

Coconut Tempura Shrimp...............................197

Cornsicles with Shrimp and Oregano 200

Creamy Pesto Shrimp.....................................203

Easy Creamed Shrimp 209

Eggplant Canoes.. 211

Fernandina Shrimp Gravy...............................214

Fried Breaded Shrimp.....................................216

Gambas al Ajillo (Garlic Shrimp) 219

Grilled Marinated Shrimp 221

Texas Shrimp...225

Hawaiian shrimp Skewers...............................227

Honey-Thyme Grilled Shrimp.........................230

Hot and Spicy Shrimp.....................................234

Italian Broiled Shrimp 237

Jerk Shrimp with Sweet Jamaican Rice...........240

Killer Shrimp 242

Lemon-Garlic Broiled Shrimp 245

Lime Pepper Shrimp.................................248

Louisiana Shrimp Esplanade...................249

Malibu Stir Fry Shrimp..........................253

Outa Sight Shrimp.................................254

Really Cool Shrimp Salad.......................257

M-80 Rock Shrimp 258

Toast of the Town................................262

Shrimp a la Plancha over Saffron Allioli Toasts
....266

Shrimp Curry..268

Shrimp in Garlic Sauce 271

Shrimp in Mustard Cream Sauce.............274

Gazpacho 278

Shrimp Marinara 283

Shrimp Newburg....................................287

Spicy Marinated Shrimp.........................290

Spicy Singapore Shrimp 292

Starlight Shrimp...................................295

Zesty Alabama Cocktail Sauce................297

Butterfly Shrimp..................................299

Cajun Shrimp..303

Chilled Aromatic Shrimp with Cilantro-Ginger-Lime Cream 305

New Orleans BBQ shrimp................................ 308

Curried Corn and Shrimp Soup........................ 311

Fiesta Shrimp...313

Pasta with Shrimp in Tomato Cream 316

Caribbean Coconut Shrimp...............................318

Papaya garlic Shrimp 320

Shrimp Creole 322

Shrimp and Grits/Classic Charleston Breakfast Shrimp 323

Biscuit Topped Seafood Gumbo Pie 327

Creamy butter shrimp.................................... 330

Prosciutto wrapped shrimp 333

Thai peanut shrimp curry............................... 336

INTRODUCTION

There are few things in life that taste as delish and divine on your tongue as a freshly cooked or an expertly prepared lobster, shrimp dish or plate of tuna. If you've never known the taste of crab or seafood that melts in your mouth, head out now and grab yourself a bite.

As a big plus, eating seafood can help prevent heart attacks and strokes, can lower blood pressure and may even help ward off depression. Regular fish consumption reduces the risk of heart attack by as much as 40 percent. Seafood's magic ingredient: omega-3 fatty acids. Fatty fish, like salmon (fresh and canned), tuna (fresh and canned), herring, trout, mackerel and sardines, are loaded with these beneficial fats. Just be careful with cooking; pan-frying and deep-frying at high temperatures can destroy omega-3 fats.

There are so many tasty ways to incorporate seafood into your meal prep. It's a healthy and delicious way to eat lean, filling protein, and a backbone of the Mediterranean diet. We are thrilled to bring you a collection of the best of the best fish and seafood recipes!

The recipes below include salmon, shrimp, scallops, octopus and Haddock. Each recipe is healthy, relatively easy to make, and full of incredible flavor. In fact, there are so many favorites here that we couldn't narrow it down. There's a little something for everyone, from shrimp fried rice to pesto salmon to perfectly seared scallops.

SHRIMP

Spicy grilled shrimp

Serves 6

Ingredients

- 1/3 cup olive oil
- 1/4 cup sesame oil
- 1/4 cup fresh parsley-chopped
- 3 Tablespoons Spicy Chipotle BBQ Sauce
- 1 Tablespoon minced garlic
- 1 Tablespoon Asian Chile Sauce
- 1 teaspoon salt
- 1 teaspoon black pepper
- 3 Tablespoons lemon juice
- 2 lbs. large shrimp, peeled and de-veined
- 12 wooden skewers, soaked in water
- Rubbing

Cooking Directions

Whisk together the olive oil, sesame oil, parsley, Spicy Chipotle BBQ Sauce, minced garlic, Chile sauce, salt, pepper, and lemon juice in a mixing bowl. Set aside about 1/3 of this marinade to use while grilling.

Place the shrimp in a large, re-sealable plastic bag. Pour in the remaining marinade and seal the bag.

Refrigerate for 2 hours. Preheat The Good-One® Grill for high heat. Thread shrimp onto skewers, piercing once near the tail and once near the head. Discard marinade.

Lightly oil grill grate. Cook shrimp for 2 minutes per side until opaque, basting frequently with reserved marinade

Grilled herbed shrimp

Serves 4

Ingredients

- 2 lbs peeled & deveined jumbo shrimp ¾ cup olive oil
- 2 tablespoons freshly squeezed lemon juice 2 cups chopped fresh basil
- 2 garlic cloves, crushed
- 1 tablespoon chopped parsley 1 teaspoon salt
- ½ teaspoon oregano
- ½ teaspoons freshly ground black pepper

Cooking Directions

5. Lay shrimp in a single layer in a shallow glass or ceramic dish.
6. In a food processor, blend the olive oil with the lemon juice.
7. Cover and refrigerate for 2 hours. Stir the shrimp 4 to 5 times during marinating.
8. Prepare the grill.
9. Lightly oil the grilling rack.
10. Lay the shrimp on the oiled rack (can skewer if desired) over the hot coals and grill for 3

to 5 minutes on each side until slightly
charred and cooked through. Do not overcook.
11. Serve immediately.

Shrimp en brochette

Serves 4 (appetizer portions)

These are great appetizers to serve before any meal. You can also substitute bay scallops. You might want to double the recipe because they are so good!

Ingredients

- $\frac{1}{2}$ tablespoon hot sauce
- 1 tablespoon Dijon-style mustard 3 tablespoons beer
- $\frac{1}{2}$ pound large shrimp, peeled and deveined 3 slices bacon, cut lengthwise into 12 strips 2 tablespoons light brown sugar

Cooking Directions

Combine the hot sauce, mustard and beer in mixing bowl.

Add the shrimp and toss to coat evenly. Refrigerate for at lest 2 hours. Drain and reserve the marinade. Wrap each shrimp with a strip of bacon.

Thread 3 shrimp onto 4 double skewers. Put the brochettes in a shallow bowl and pour in the reserved marinade. Sprinkle the shrimp with the sugar. Refrigerate for at least 1 hour.

Prepare Good-One Grill. Place the brochettes on the grill, pour the marinade over them, and close the lid. Cook for 4 minutes, then turn them over, close the lid and cook for 4 minutes.

Serve immediately

Shrimp packets

- 4 lbs Large Shrimp
- 1 Cup Butter or Margarine
- 1 Large Clove Garlic, Minced
- 1/2 tsp black pepper
- 1 tsp salt
- 1 cup parsley, minced

Peel and clean shrimp

Cream butter; add remaining ingredients to the butter and mix well. Cut 6 (9-inch) strips of heavy duty aluminum foil. Then cut each strip in half. Divide shrimp equally on each piece of foil. Top each with 1/12th of the butter mixture, bring foil up around shrimp; twist tightly to seal. Place shrimp packets on embers. Cook 5 minutes.

Makes 12 packets

Basil shrimp

- 2 1/2 tablespoons olive oil
- 1/4 cup butter, melted
- 1/2 lemons, juiced
- tablespoons coarse grained prepared mustard

- ounces minced fresh basil
- cloves garlic, minced
- salt to taste
- 1 pinch white pepper
- 3 pounds fresh shrimp, peeled and deveined

In a shallow, non-porous dish or bowl, mix together olive oil and melted butter. Then stir in lemon juice, mustard, basil and garlic, and season with salt and white pepper. Add shrimp, and toss to coat. Cover, and place in refrigerator or cooler for 1 hour. Preheat grill to high heat. Remove shrimp from marinade, and thread on skewers. Lightly oil grate, and arrange skewers on grill. Cook for 4 minutes, turning once, until done.

Grilled bacon-wrapped shrimp

- 1 lb. large shrimp
- bacon slices, cut in 1/2
- pepper jack cheese

Wash, shell, and devein shrimp. Slit the back of each shrimp. Place a small slice of cheese in the slit and wrap with a piece of bacon. Use a toothpick to hold together. Cook on the grill until bacon is slightly crisp. This is delicious and easy!

Grilled shrimp

- 1 pound medium sized shrimp
- 3-4 tablespoons olive oil
- 2 tablespoons "Old Bay Seasoning"

Peel and devein shrimp, leaving on the tails. Place all ingredients in a zip lock bag and shake well. This can marinade 5 minutes or several hours. Place shrimp on a "grill pan" (with holes so that the shrimp do not fall in between grates on the grill) and grill medium high for several minutes. Very spicy

Serves 2

Alabama Shrimp Bake

- 1 cup butter or margarine, melted
- 3/4 cup lemon juice
- 3/4 cup Worcestershire sauce
- 1 tablespoon salt
- 1 tablespoon coarsely ground pepper
- 1 teaspoon dried rosemary
- 1/8 teaspoon ground red pepper
- 1 tablespoon hot sauce
- 3 garlic cloves, minced
- 2 1/2 pounds unpeeled large or jumbo shrimp
- 2 lemons, thinly sliced
- 1 medium onion, thinly sliced
- Fresh rosemary sprigs

Combine first 9 ingredients in a small bowl; set aside.

Rinse shrimp with cold water; drain well. Layer shrimp, lemon slices, and onion slices in an ungreased 13 x 9 x 2-inch baking dish. Pour butter mixture over shrimp. Bake uncovered, at 400 degrees F for 20 to 25 minutes or until shrimp turn pink, basting occasionally with pan juices. Garnish with fresh rosemary sprigs.

Serves 6.

Almost Shrimp Paesano

- Shrimp
- 1 egg
- 1 cup milk
- Salt and pepper to taste
- 1 pound extra-large shrimp, peeled and deveined, tails left on
- 1/2 cup all-purpose flour
- Vegetable oil

In a shallow bowl, combine eggs, milk, salt and pepper. Dip shrimp in mixture, then dip in flour lightly.

Heat oil in a sauté pan until hot, and then add shrimp 4 to 6 at a time, making sure shrimp have plenty of room to cook. (It's important that shrimp are not near each other or touch.) Brown them on one side, then turn and brown them on the other. Cook until done, or put on a baking sheet in a preheated 350 degrees F oven to finish cooking. Meanwhile, prepare sauce.

Sauce

- 1 1/2 cups (3 sticks) cold butter, cut into 1-inch pieces
- Juice of 1 medium lemon
- 1 clove garlic, minced
- 2 tablespoons minced fresh parsley

In a heavy saucepan, combine butter, lemon juice and garlic. Put over medium-low heat and whisk mixture constantly until the butter is just melted and thickened. Stir in parsley, then remove from heat.

Pool sauce on plate, then top with cooked shrimp

Serves 3 to 4

Bean & Shrimp Risotto

- 1 ½ cups onion, chopped
- 1 lb. peeled, deveined shrimp
- 4 cloves garlic, minced
- 1 cup snap peas
- 1 TBS olive oil
- 1 can kidney beans or ½ cups cooked
- 3 to 4oz. mushrooms, sliced
- dry-package kidney beans, rinsed,
- 1 ½ cups Arborio rice, drained
- 3 cans fat-free reduced-sodium chicken broth
- 1 medium tomato, chopped
- cup Parmesan or Asiago cheese
- salt & pepper to taste

Sauté' onion, garlic, & mushrooms in oil in large saucepan until tender, 5 to 8 Minutes.

Stir in rice and cook 2 to 3 Minutes.

Heat broth to boiling in medium saucepan; reduce heat to low. Add 1 cup broth to rice and cook, stirring constantly, until broth is absorbed, 1 to 2

Minutes. Slowly add 2 cups broth and simmer, stirring, until broth is absorbed.

Add shrimp, snap peas and remaining broth to saucepan. Cook, stirring frequently, until rice is just tender and liquid is absorbed, 5 to 10 Minutes. Add beans and tomatoes; cook 2 to 3 Minutes longer. Stir in cheese; season to taste with salt & pepper.

Beer-Broiled Shrimp

- 3/4 cup Beer
- 3 tablespoons vegetable oil
- 2 tablespoons snipped parsley
- 4 teaspoons Worcestershire sauce
- 1 clove garlic, minced
- 1/2 teaspoon salt
- 1/8 teaspoon pepper
- 2 pounds large shrimp, unshelled

Combine Coors®, oil, parsley, Worcestershire sauce, garlic, salt and pepper. Add shrimp; stir. Cover; let stand at room temperature for 1 hour.

Drain, reserving marinade. Place shrimp on well-greased broiler rack; broil 4 to 5 inches from heat for 4 minutes. Turn; brush with marinade. Broil 2 to 4 minutes more or until bright pink.

Makes 6 servings

Boiled Gulf Shrimp

- 1 gallon water
- 1 (3 ounce) box Zatarain's crab boil

- 2 lemons, sliced
- 6peppercorns
- 2bay leaves
- 5pounds raw shrimp in the shell

Bring to boil the water seasoned with crab boil, lemons, peppercorns and bay leaves. Drop in shrimp. When water returns to a boil, cook jumbo or large shrimp for 12 to 13 minutes and medium shrimp for 7 to 8 minutes. Remove from heat and add 1 quart ice water. Let sit for 10 minutes. Drain.

Serve Rémoulade Sauce as a dip.

Rémoulade Sauce

- 1/2 tablespoon Creole mustard or more
- 2 tablespoons grated onion
- 1 pint mayonnaise
- 1/4 cup horseradish or more
- 1/2 cup chopped chives
- 1/4 teaspoon salt
- 1 tablespoon lemon juice
- 1/4 teaspoon pepper

Mix all ingredients. Serve over cold boiled shrimp for a shrimp rémoulade main course or use as a dip for boiled shrimp. Sauce is best after 24 hours.

Makes 2 1/4 cups sauce.

California Scampi

- 1 pound butter, clarified
- 1 tablespoon minced garlic
- 1 teaspoon salt
- 1 teaspoon pepper
- 1 1/2 pounds large shrimp, shelled and de-veined

Heat 3 tablespoons of the clarified butter in a large skillet. Add garlic and sauté. Add salt and pepper and the shrimp, which can be butterflied, if desired. Sauté until shrimp change color and are tender. Add remaining butter and heat through. Place shrimp on plates and spoon hot butter over.

Makes 4 to 6 servings

Champagne Shrimp And Pasta

- 8 ounces angel hair pasta
- 1 tablespoon extra-virgin olive oil
- 1 cup sliced fresh mushrooms
- 1 pound medium shrimp, peeled and deveined
- 1-1/2 cups champagne
- 1/4 teaspoon salt
- 2 tablespoons minced shallots
- 2 plum tomatoes, diced
- 1 cup heavy cream
- salt and pepper to taste
- 3 tablespoons chopped fresh parsley
- freshly grated Parmesan cheese

Bring a large pot of lightly salted water to a boil. Cook pasta in boiling water for 6 to 8 minutes or until al dente; drain. Meanwhile, heat oil over medium-high heat in a large frying pan. Cook and stir mushrooms in oil until tender. Remove mushrooms from pan, and set aside.

Combine shrimp, champagne, and salt in the frying pan, and cook over high heat. When liquid just begins to boil, remove shrimp from pan. Add shallots and tomatoes to champagne; boil until liquid is reduced to 1/2 cup, about 8 minutes. Stir in 3/4 cup cream; boil until slightly thick, about 1 to 2 minutes. Add shrimp and mushrooms to sauce, and heat through. Adjust seasonings to taste. Toss hot, cooked pasta with remaining 1/4 cup cream and parsley. To serve, spoon shrimp with sauce over pasta, and top with Parmesan cheese.

Coconut Shrimp with Jalapeño Jelly

- 3 cups shredded coconut
- 12 (16–20 or 26–30) shrimp, peeled and deveined
- 1 cup flour
- 2 eggs, beaten
- Vegetable oil

Lightly toast the coconut on a cookie sheet in a 350 degrees F oven for 8 to 10 minutes.

Butterfly each shrimp by splitting lengthwise down the center, cutting three-fourths of the way through. Dredge the shrimp in flour and then dip in egg. Press the shredded coconut into the shrimp and then fry in 350 degrees F vegetable oil until golden brown.

Serve with Jalapeño Jelly.

Jalapeño Jelly

- 1 cup red wine vinegar
- 1 cup water
- 1 cup granulated sugar
- 2 green jalapeño peppers, seeded and minced

- 1 small red bell pepper, minced
- 1 package liquid pectin

Place all ingredients, except pectin, in a saucepan and bring to a boil. Add the pectin and bring to a boil again. Remove from heat and cool.

The Jalapeño Jelly can be stored in an airtight container in the refrigerator for 7 to 14 days.

Coconut Tempura Shrimp

- 2/3 cup flour
- 1/2 cup cornstarch
- 1 large egg, beaten
- 1 cup grated fresh coconut
- 1 cup ice-cold soda water
- Salt
- 1 pound large shrimp, peeled, deveined, and tail on
- Creole seasoning
- 1 jar mango chutney
- 1 plantain
- 1 tablespoon cilantro, finely chopped

Preheat the fryer.

In a medium-size mixing bowl, combine the flour, cornstarch, egg, coconut, and soda water. Mix well to make a smooth batter. Season with salt. Season the shrimp with Creole seasoning. Holding the tail of the shrimp, dip in the batter, coating completely and shaking off the excess. Fry the shrimp in batches until golden brown, about 4 to 6 minutes. Remove and drain on paper towels. Season with Creole seasoning.

Peel the plantains. Slice the plantains thinly, lengthwise. Fry them until golden brown. Remove and drain on paper towels. Season with Creole seasoning.

Mound some mango chutney in the center of each plate. Lay the shrimp around the chutney. Garnish with fried plantains and cilantro.

Cornsicles with Shrimp and Oregano

- 6 ears corn
- 1 teaspoon salt
- 1/4 teaspoon white pepper
- 1 tablespoon chopped fresh Mexican oregano or
- 1 teaspoon dried Mexican oregano
- 12 medium shrimp
- 24 Popsicle sticks

Peel, devein and dice shrimp. Trim the corn and remove the husks and silk. Save and wash the larger husks. Cut the corn kernels from the cob, scraping out as much milk as you can. Grind the kernels using a meat grinder with a sharp blade. Add the salt, white pepper, oregano and shrimp. Mix well.

Preheat oven to 325 degrees F.

Drop a tablespoon of the corn mixture onto the center of a clean husk. Fold the left side of the husk into the center, then the right, and then fold the bottom end upward. Push a Popsicle stick 2 to 3 inches into the open end and pinch the husk around the stick with your fingers. Tear a thin strand from a dry husk and tie it around the cornsicle. Place the rolls, sticks in the air and very close together, in a glass baking dish or loaf pan. Bake 30 minutes, until the corn mixture is firm and solid.

To eat a cornsicle, peel off the corn husk and eat it hot from the stick, as you would a Popsicle.

Creamy Pesto Shrimp

- 1 pound linguine pasta
- 1/2 cup butter
- 2 cups heavy cream
- 1/2 teaspoon ground black pepper
- 1 cup grated Parmesan cheese
- 1/3 cup pesto (recipe follows)
- 1 pound large shrimp, peeled and deveined

Bring a large pot of lightly salted water to a boil. Add linguine pasta, and cook for 8 to 10 minutes, or until al dente; drain. In a large skillet, melt

the butter over medium heat. Stir in cream, and season with pepper. Cook 6 to 8 minutes, stirring constantly. Stir Parmesan cheese into cream sauce, stirring until thoroughly mixed. Blend in the pesto, and cook for 3 to 5 minutes, until thickened. Stir in the shrimp, and cook until they turn pink, about 5 minutes. Serve over the hot linguine.

Pesto Sauce:

- 1 1/2 cups packed tender young basil leaves
- 2 heaping tablespoons pine nuts
- 1 teaspoon coarse salt

- 1/4 cup extra-virgin olive oil or more to taste 2 garlic cloves, very finely minced
- 1/4 cup freshly grated Parmigiano cheese

Put the basil, pine nuts, and salt in a food processor or blender and process steadily while you add the oil in a thin but constant stream. The sauce should achieve the consistency of a slightly grainy paste but not a fine puree. Add the garlic and process very briefly, just to mix. When the sauce is the right consistency, transfer it to a bowl and, using a spatula, fold in the grated cheese. (If you're using a mortar, just continue to work in the cheese with the pestle.) If the sauce is too thick, work in more olive oil. Taste and adjust the seasoning.

Delta Shrimp

- 2 quarts water
- 1/2 large lemon, sliced
- 2 1/2 pounds unpeeled large fresh shrimp
- 1 cup vegetable oil
- 2 tablespoons hot sauce
- 1 1/2 teaspoons olive oil
- 1 1/2 teaspoons minced garlic
- 1 teaspoon minced fresh parsley
- 3/4 teaspoon salt
- 3/4 teaspoon Old Bay® seasoning
- 3/4 teaspoon dried whole basil
- 3/4 teaspoon dried whole oregano
- 3/4 teaspoon dried whole thyme
- Leaf lettuce

Bring water and lemon to a boil; add shrimp and cook 3 to 5 minutes. Drain well; rinse with cold water. Peel and devein shrimp, leaving tails intact. Place shrimp in a large bowl.

Combine oil and next 9 ingredients; stir with a wire whisk. Pour over shrimp. Toss to coat shrimp.

Easy Creamed Shrimp

- 3 cans cream of shrimp soup
- 1 1/2 teaspoons curry powder
- 3 cups sour cream
- 1 1/2 pounds shrimp, cooked and peeled

Combine all ingredients and heat in top of double boiler.

Serve over rice or in patty shells.

Eggplant Canoes

- 4 medium eggplants
- 1 cup onions, chopped
- 1 cup green onions, chopped
- 4 cloves garlic, chopped
- 1 cup bell pepper, chopped
- 1/2 cup celery, chopped
- 2 bay leaves
- 1 teaspoon thyme
- 4 teaspoons salt
- 1 teaspoon black pepper
- 4 tablespoons bacon grease
- 1 1/2 pounds raw shrimp, peeled
- 1/2 cup (1 stick) butter
- 1 tablespoon Worcestershire sauce
- 1 teaspoon Louisiana hot sauce
- 1 cup seasoned Italian bread crumbs
- 2 eggs, beaten
- 1/2 cup parsley, chopped
- 1 pound lump crabmeat
- 3 tablespoons lemon juice
- 8 tablespoons Romano cheese, grated
- 1 cup sharp Cheddar cheese, grated

Cut eggplants in half lengthwise and boil in salted water for about 10 minutes or until tender. Scoop out insides and chop finely. Place eggplant shells in a shallow baking dish. Sauté onions, green onions, garlic, bell pepper, celery, bay leaves, thyme, salt and pepper in bacon grease for about 15 to 20 minutes. Add chopped eggplant and cook covered for about 30 minutes.

In a separate skillet, sauté shrimp in butter until they turn pink, about 2 minutes, then add to eggplant mixture. Add Worcestershire sauce, hot sauce, bread crumbs and eggs to eggplant mixture. Stir in parsley and lemon juice. Add cheese. Gently fold in crabmeat. Fill eggplant shells with mixture. Bake uncovered at 350 degrees F until hot and browned, about 30 minutes.

Yields 8 servings

Fernandina Shrimp Gravy

- 1 tablespoon granulated sugar
- 1 tablespoon plus 1 cup water
- 2 ounces salt pork, diced
- 1/2 cup minced onion
- 1/2 cup diced green bell pepper
- 1/2 cup diced red bell pepper
- 1/2 cup diced celery
- 1 1/2 pounds shrimp, shelled, cleaned and, if large, cut into pieces
- 1 teaspoon salt
- 1/4 teaspoon freshly-ground black pepper
- 1/8 teaspoon crushed dried red pepper
- 2 cups hot cooked rice

In a heavy, medium-size skillet, stir the sugar over moderate heat until it begins to melt. Continue to cook until the syrup turns golden. Add the tablespoon of water, protecting your hands with a pot holder as the hot sugar may spatter. Stir until the sugar is dissolved. Set this caramel aside.

In a large skillet or sauté pan, cook the salt pork until browned, stirring now and then. Remove the pork bits with a slotted spoon, and set aside. Pour off all but 1 tablespoon of pork drippings. Add the onion, green and red peppers and celery. Sauté until the vegetables are tender. Add the shrimp and cook until they turn bright pink and are opaque, 2 to 3 minutes. Remove the shrimp and vegetables with a slotted spoon and keep them warm on a plate. Add the remaining 1 cup water and 1 teaspoon of the caramel to the pan drippings. Bring to a boil, stir, and simmer 1 to 2 minutes. Season with salt, black pepper and crushed red pepper. Return the shrimp and vegetables and the salt pork bits to the gravy and heat a minute or two.

Serve hot over rice.

Fried Breaded Shrimp

1/4 cup flour
Salt and pepper
1egg
2tablespoons vodka
3/4 cup fine bread crumbs
40 large raw shrimp, shelled, but with tails intact
Oil (for frying)

Mix flour with a little salt and pepper and place in a bowl. In a second bowl beat well the egg and vodka. In a third bowl place the bread crumbs mixed with salt and pepper. Toss the shrimp, one at a time, in the flour; dip into egg mixture; toss in the bread crumbs to coat. Drop into hot oil (360 degrees

and deep fry quickly until golden brown. Do not overcook. Shrimp may be breaded several hours ahead and refrigerated until time to fry. Serve with a tartar and a cocktail sauce.

Serves 3 to 4.

Gambas al Ajillo (Garlic Shrimp)

- 2 tablespoons olive oil
- 4 cloves garlic, sliced thinly
- 1 tablespoon crushed red pepper (or 3 guindilla peppers, crushed)
- 1 pound shrimp
- salt and pepper, to taste

Heat the olive oil in a skillet on medium heat. Add the garlic and red pepper. Saute until the garlic is browned, stirring often to make sure the garlic doesn't burn.

Toss the shrimp in the oil (be careful that the oil doesn't splash up on you). Cook for 2 minutes on each side, until pink.
Add the salt and pepper. Cook for another minute before removing from the heat. Serve with slices of baguette (tapas-style) or with pasta.

If you're tossing with pasta:

Start in a large saucepan. Cook shrimp as instructed, while making pasta in a separate pot (you will probably start the pasta before the shrimp, since the shrimp only takes 5-7 minutes) . While draining the pasta, reserve some of the pasta water. When the shrimp is finished, pour the cooked pasta into the saucepan with the shrimp and toss well, coating the pasta with the garlic and red pepper-infused oil. Add reserved pasta water, in tablespoon increments, if necessary. Top with chopped parsley.

Grilled Marinated Shrimp

Ingredients

1 cup olive oil
1/4 cup chopped fresh parsley
1 lemon, juiced
2 tablespoons hot pepper sauce
3 cloves garlic, minced
1 tablespoon tomato paste
2 teaspoons dried oregano
1 teaspoon salt
1 teaspoon ground black pepper
2 pounds large shrimp, peeled and deveined with
tails attached
Skewers

Directions

In a mixing bowl, mix together olive oil, parsley,
lemon juice, hot sauce, garlic, tomato paste,
oregano, salt, and black pepper. Reserve a small
amount for basting later. Pour remaining marinade
into a large resealable plastic bag with shrimp.
Seal, and marinate in the refrigerator for 2 hours.

Preheat grill for medium-low heat. Thread shrimp onto skewers, piercing once near the tail and once near the head. Discard marinade.

Lightly oil grill grate. Cook shrimp for 5 minutes per side, or until opaque, basting frequently with reserved marinade.

Texas Shrimp

- 1/4 cup vegetable oil
- 1/4 cup tequila
- 1/4 cup red wine vinegar
- 2 tablespoons Mexican lime juice
- 1 tablespoon ground red chiles
- 1/2 teaspoon salt
- 2 cloves garlic, finely chopped
- 1 red bell pepper, finely chopped
- 24 large raw shrimp, peeled and de-veined (tails left on)

Mix all ingredients except shrimp in shallow glass or plastic dish. Stir in shrimp. Cover and refrigerate for 1 hour.

Remove shrimp from marinade, reserving marinade. Thread 4 shrimp on each of six (8-inch) metal skewers. Grill over medium coals, turning once, until pink, 2 to 3 minutes on each side.

Heat marinade to boiling in a nonreactive saucepan. Reduce heat to low. Simmer uncovered until bell pepper is tender, about 5 minutes. Serve with shrimp.

Makes 6 servings

NOTE: If you would prefer to broil the shrimp instead of grilling them, place the skewered shrimp on a broiler pan rack. Broil with tops about 4 inches from heat, turning once, until pink, 2 to 3 minutes on each side.

Hawaiian shrimp Skewers

- 1/2 pound shrimp, peeled, deveined & uncooked 1/2 pound bay or sea scallops 1 can pineapple chunks in juice
- 1 green bell pepper, cut in wedges
- bacon slices

Sauce:

- 6 ounces barbecue sauce
- 16 ounces salsa
- 2 tablespoons pineapple juice
- 2 tablespoons white wine

Blend sauce ingredients until evenly mixed. Skewer pineapple chunks, shrimp, scallops, bell pepper wedges, and bacon slices folded. Baste skewer evenly on each side and grill. Cook until shrimp are a pink color. Serve with rice.

Honey-Thyme Grilled Shrimp

Roasted Garlic Marinade

2 pounds fresh or frozen uncooked large shrimp in shells

1 medium red bell pepper, cut into 1-inch squares and blanched

1 medium yellow bell pepper, cut into 1-inch squares and blanched

1 medium red onion, cut into quarters and separated into chunks

Prepare Roasted Garlic Marinade (recipe follows).

Peel shrimp. (If shrimp are frozen, do not thaw; peel in cold water.) Make a shallow cut lengthwise down back of each shrimp; wash out vein.

Pour 1/2 cup of the marinade into small resealable plastic bag; seal bag and refrigerate until serving. Pour remaining marinade into large resealable plastic bag. Add shrimp, bell peppers and onion, turning to coat with marinade. Seal bag and refrigerate at least 2 hours but no longer than 24 hours.

Brush grill rack with vegetable oil. Heat coals or gas grill for direct heat. Remove shrimp and vegetables from marinade; drain well. Discard marinade. Thread shrimp and vegetables alternately on each of six 15-inch metal skewers, leaving space between each.

Grill kabobs uncovered 4 to 6 inches from HOT heat 7 to 10 minutes, turning once, until shrimp are pink and firm. Place kabobs on serving tray. Cut a tiny corner from small plastic bag of reserved marinade, using scissors. Drizzle marinade over shrimp and vegetables.

Yield: 6 servings.

Roasted Garlic Marinade

1 medium bulb garlic

1/3 cup olive or vegetable oil

2/3 cup orange juice

1/4 cup spicy honey mustard

3 tablespoons honey

3/4 teaspoon dried thyme leaves, crushed

Preheat oven to 375 degrees F.Cut one-third off top of unpeeled garlic bulb, exposing cloves. Place garlic in small baking dish; drizzle with oil. Cover tightly and bake 45 minutes; cool. Squeeze garlic pulp from papery skin. Place garlic and remaining ingredients in blender. Cover and blend on high speed until smooth. Makes about 1 1/2 cups.

Hot and Spicy Shrimp

1 pound butter

1/4 cup peanut oil

3 cloves garlic, chopped

2 tablespoons rosemary

1 teaspoon chopped basil

1 teaspoon chopped thyme

1 teaspoon chopped oregano

1 small hot pepper, chopped, or

2 tablespoons ground cayenne pepper

2 teaspoons fresh ground black pepper

2 bay leaves, crumbled

1 tablespoon paprika

2 teaspoons lemon juice

2 pounds raw shrimp in their shells

Salt

Shrimp should be of a size to number 30–35 per pound.

Melt the butter and oil in a flameproof baking dish. Add the garlic, herbs, peppers, bay leaves, paprika, and lemon juice, and bring to a boil. Turn the heat down and simmer 10 minutes, stirring frequently. Remove the dish from the heat and let the flavors marry at least 30 minutes.

This hot butter sauce can be made a day in advance and refrigerated. Preheat the oven to 450 degrees F. Reheat the sauce, add the shrimp, and cook over medium heat until the shrimp just turn pink, then bake in the oven about 30 minutes more. Taste for seasoning, adding salt if necessary. Sop up butter sauce with crusty bread after the shrimp have been eaten.

Italian Broiled Shrimp

2 pounds jumbo shrimp

1/4 cup olive oil

2 tablespoons garlic, minced

1/4 cup flour

1/4 cup butter, melted

4 tablespoons parsley, minced

1 cup Drawn Butter Sauce

Shell shrimp, leaving tails on. Dry, then dust with flour. Stir oil and butter into flat baking dish; add shrimp. Broil at medium heat for 8 minutes. Add garlic and parsley to Drawn Butter Sauce. Pour over shrimp. Stir until shrimp are coated. Broil 2 more minutes.

Jerk Shrimp with Sweet Jamaican Rice

1 pound medium shrimp (51–60 count), raw, shell on
Jerk seasoning

2 cups hot cooked rice

1 (11 ounce) can mandarin oranges, drained and
chopped

1 (8 ounce) can crushed pineapple, drained

1/2 cup chopped red bell pepper

1/4 cup slivered almonds, toasted

1/2 cup sliced scallions

2 tablespoons flaked coconut, toasted

1/4 teaspoon ground ginger

Prepare jerk marinade according to package
instructions on back of jerk seasoning.

Peel and devein shrimp leaving the tail on. Place in
marinade while preparing rice.

In large skillet, combine all remaining ingredients. Cook over medium-high heat, stirring constantly for 5 minutes or until thoroughly heated. Remove shrimp from marinade. Place in broiler pan in single layer. Broil 5 to 6 inches from heat for 2 minutes.

Stir well and broil an additional 2 minutes or until shrimp are just pink.

Serve with rice.

Killer Shrimp

2 tablespoons dried rosemary

2 teaspoons dried thyme

1/2 teaspoon fennel seed

1 teaspoon black pepper

5 cloves garlic, peeled and chopped

1 teaspoon celery seed

1 teaspoon crushed red pepper flakes

2 quarts low-sodium chicken broth

8 ounces clam juice

3 ounces tomato paste

1/2 cup (1 stick) butter

1 cup white wine

1 1/2 pounds raw peeled shrimp, with tails

French bread (for dipping)

Partially break up the rosemary, thyme, and fennel seed with fingers or mortar and pestle.

Place all ingredients, except wine and shrimp, in a large pot. Simmer for about 30 minutes, then add wine. Continue to simmer for a total cooking time of no more than 2 hours.

Just before serving, add raw shrimp. Simmer until shrimp is done, stirring, about 2 minutes.

Each bowl should contain a serving of shrimp and a lot of broth, which should almost completely cover the shrimp. The dish is eaten with your fingers. Soak up the broth with the bread.

Yields 4 servings.

Lemon–Garlic Broiled Shrimp

2 pounds medium shrimp, peeled and deveined
2 cloves garlic, halved
1/4 cup butter or margarine, melted
1/2 teaspoon salt
Coarse ground pepper
3 drops hot sauce
1 tablespoon Worcestershire sauce
5 tablespoons chopped fresh parsley

Place shrimp in single layer in a 15 x 10 x 1-inch jellyroll pan; set aside.
Sauté garlic in butter until garlic is browned; remove and discard garlic. Add remaining ingredients, except parsley, stirring well. Pour mixture over shrimp. Broil shrimp4 inches from heat for 8 to 10 minutes, basting once. Sprinkle with parsley.
Yields 6 servings.

Lime Pepper Shrimp

1 pound large shrimp, peeled and deveined
1 tablespoon olive oil
1 Tablespoon minced fresh rosemary
1 tablespoon minced fresh thyme
2 teaspoons minced garlic
1 teaspoon coarsely-ground black pepper
Pinch of ground red pepper
Juice of one lime

In a medium bowl, combine the shrimp, oil, herbs and peppers. Mix well to coat the shrimp. Let stand at room temperature for 20 minutes.

Heat a large no-stick frying pan over medium-high heat for 3 minutes. Add the shrimp in a single layer. Cook for 3 minutes per side, or until the shrimp a pink and just cooked through. Do not overcook. Remove from heat and stir in lime juice.

Louisiana Shrimp Esplanade

24 large fresh shrimp
12 ounces butter
1 tablespoon puréed garlic
2 tablespoons Worcestershire sauce
1 teaspoon dried thyme
1 teaspoon dried rosemary
1/2 teaspoon dried oregano
1/2 teaspoon crushed red pepper
1 teaspoon cayenne pepper
1 teaspoon black pepper
8 ounces beer
4 cups cooked white rice
1/2 cup finely chopped scallions

Wash shrimp and leave in the shell. Melt butter in a large frying pan and stir in the garlic, Worcestershire sauce and seasonings.
Add shrimp and shake the pan to immerse the shrimp in butter, then sauté over medium-high heat for 4 to 5 minutes until they turn pink. Next, pour in the beer and stir for a further minute, then remove from the heat. Shell and devein the shrimp and arrange on a bed of rice. Pour the pan juices on top and garnish with chopped scallion.

Serve immediately.

Malibu Stir Fry Shrimp

1 tablespoon peanut oil
1 tablespoon butter
1 tablespoon minced garlic
1 pound medium shrimp, shelled and deveined
1 cup sliced mushrooms
1 bunch scallions, sliced
1 red sweet pepper, seeded, cut in thin 2" strips
1 cup fresh or frozen peas
1 cup Malibu rum
1 cup heavy cream
1/4 cup chopped fresh basil or 1 tablespoon dried
2 teaspoons ground chili paste or 2 tablespoons
prepared chili sauce
Juice of 1/2 lime
Fresh ground black pepper
1/2 cup shredded coconut
1 pound fettuccini, cooked
Heat oil and butter over high heat in large pan.
Add garlic for 1 minute. Add shrimp, cook 2
minutes until pink. Add vegetables and fry 2
minutes. Add rum and simmer 2 minutes. Add
cream and simmer 5 minutes. Add remaining
seasonings. Toss with coconut and cooked pasta.

Outa Sight Shrimp

4 pounds unpeeled, large fresh shrimp or 6 pound
shrimp with heads on
1/2 cup butter
1/2 cup olive oil
1/4 cup chili sauce
1/4 cup Worcestershire sauce
2 lemons, sliced
4 garlic cloves, chopped
2 tablespoons Creole seasoning
2 tablespoons lemon juice
1 tablespoon chopped parsley
1 teaspoon paprika
1 teaspoon oregano
1 teaspoon ground red pepper
1/2 teaspoon hot sauce
French bread
Spread shrimp in a shallow, aluminum foil-lined
broiler pan. Combine butter and next 12
ingredients in a saucepan over low heat, stirring
until butter melts, and pour over shrimp. Cover and
chill 2 hours, turning shrimp every 30 minutes.

Bake, uncovered, at 400 degrees F for 20 minutes;
turn once.

Serve with bread, green salad and corn on the cob
for a complete meal.

Really Cool Shrimp Salad

2 Lbs. Medium Shrimp

1 Cup Miracle Whip

1/2 Cup Green Onions

1 Green Bell Pepper

1 Small Head of Lettuce

1 Medium Tomato

1/2 Cup Mozzarella Cheese

Peel, devein, and boil shrimp. Chop lettuce, bell pepper, tomato, green onions and shrimp, and mix together in bowl... Shred mozzarella cheese and add to salad.. Add miracle whip and mix together well. Refrigerate for at least one hour and serve by itself or with your favorite seafood meal.....

M-80 Rock Shrimp

M-80 Sauce

- 1 tablespoon cornstarch
- 1 cup water
- 1 cup soy sauce
- 1 cup light brown sugar
- 1 tablespoon sambal chile paste
- cup freshly squeezed orange juice 1 serrano chile, finely chopped
- cloves garlic, finely chopped (about 1 tablespoon)
- One two-inch piece fresh ginger, scraped/peeled and finely chopped

Slaw

- head green cabbage, thinly sliced (about 1½ cups)
- head red cabbage, thinly sliced (about 1½ cups)
- medium carrot, thinly sliced into 2-inch pieces
- medium red pepper, thinly sliced
- medium red onion, thinly sliced
- 1 garlic clove, thinly sliced
- 1 Serrano chile, thinly sliced

- basil leaves, thinly sliced

Shrimp

- Vegetable oil
- 2 pound rock shrimp (or substitute 16-20 count shrimp cut into small cubes) 1 cup buttermilk
- 3 cup all-purpose flour
- Black and white sesame seeds
- 1 tablespoon green onions, thinly sliced
- Cilantro leaves

Make the M-80 sauce: In a small bowl, whisk together the cornstarch and water. Set aside. In a small saucepan, whisk together the soy sauce, brown sugar, chile paste, orange juice, chile, garlic and ginger and bring the sauce to a boil. Lower the heat and simmer for 15 minutes. Whisk in the cornstarch-water mixture and bring the sauce back up to a boil.

Make the slaw: In a medium bowl, toss together the green and red cabbage, carrot, red pepper, onion, garlic, chile and basil. Set aside.

Make the shrimp: In a medium saucepan set over high heat, add enough oil to come halfway up the pot; heat until the oil reaches 350° (use a thermometer to measure the temperature). Put the rock shrimp in a large bowl and pour the buttermilk over them. Use a slotted spoon to remove the shrimp, drain off the excess buttermilk and, in a separate bowl, toss the shrimp with the flour. Fry the shrimp for 1 to $1\frac{1}{2}$ Minutes.

Toast of the Town

INGREDIENTS

Twelve 16-20 count shrimp, deveined and shells removed

Salt and freshly ground black pepper

avocados

tablespoons lime juice (about 1 medium lime), divided

tablespoons finely chopped cilantro

teaspoons finely chopped jalapeño (about 1 medium jalapeño)

1 grapefruit

1 small baguette, sliced into $\frac{1}{4}$-inch slices Extra-virgin olive oil

Salt and freshly ground black pepper $\frac{1}{4}$ cup pistachios, toasted and chopped

DIRECTIONS

Place the shrimp on a small plate and season with salt and pepper. Cut the avocados lengthwise around the pits and remove the pits. Cut the avocado flesh in a crosshatch pattern and use a spoon to scoop the avocado flesh into a medium bowl. Combine the avocado with $1\frac{1}{2}$ tablespoons of the lime juice and the cilantro and jalapeño.

Use a knife to remove the skin and any pith from the grapefruit flesh and slice along the membranes to remove the segments. Set aside.

Brush the baguette slices with olive oil and season with salt and pepper. Place the baguette slices in the toaster and toast until golden brown.

In a medium skillet set over medium heat, heat $1\frac{1}{2}$ tablespoons of olive oil and add the shrimp. Cook for one minute on one side, then flip and cook an additional 30 seconds on the other side. Transfer the shrimp to a bowl and toss with the remaining $\frac{1}{2}$ tablespoon of lime juice.

To assemble: Spread 2 tablespoons of avocado mixture on each baguette slice. Top with one or two pieces of shrimp and a segment of grapefruit. Sprinkle pistachios over the top and serve immediately.

Shrimp Curry with Mustard

The unique combination of shrimps and mustard is a culinary delight.

Ingredients:

- 1 lb. shrimps
- 2 tbsp. oil
- 1 tsp. turmeric
- 2 tbsp. mustard powder
- 1 tsp. salt
- 8 green chillies

Method:

Make a paste of mustard in an equal amount of water. Heat oil in a non-stick frying pan and fry the mustard paste and the shrimps for at least five minutes, and add 2 cups of lukewarm water.

Bring to a boil and add turmeric and salt and green chillies. Cook on medium low heat foranother twenty five minutes.

Shrimp Curry

Ingredients:

- 1 lb. shrimps, peeled and deveined
- 1 onion, pureed
- 1 tsp. ginger paste
- 1 tsp. garlic paste
- 1 tomato, pureed
- 1 tsp. turmeric powder
- 1 tsp. chilli powder
- 1 tsp. cumin powder
- 1 tsp. coriander powder
- 1 tsp. salt or to taste
- 1 tsp. lemon juice
- Cilantro/coriander leaves
- 1 tbsp. oil

Method:

Heat oil in a non-stick frying pan and fry the onion, tomato, ginger and garlic, together with cumin and coriander powders and cilantro/coriander leaves for five minutes on medium low heat. Add shrimp, turmeric and chili powders and salt together with half a cup of lukewarm water and cook on medium low heat for twenty five minutes. Keep the pan covered with a lid. Stir well to let the shrimps blend with the spices. Season with lemon juice, garnish with cilantro/coriander before serving.

Note: Using pre-cooked, peeled and deveined shrimp available in the grocery store to reduce preparation time.

Shrimp in Garlic Sauce

12 cloves garlic, roughly chopped

1 cup vegetable oil

1/4 cup (1/2 stick) unsalted butter

1 1/2 pounds fresh shrimp, peeled, de-veinedand butterflied (leave tails intact)

In a large skillet, sauté the garlic in medium-hot oil (about 300 degrees F) until light brown. Watch carefully so as not to burn. After about 6 to 8 minutes, quickly whisk in the butter and remove immediately from the fire. When all the butter has been added, the bits will become crisp. Remove them with a slotted spoon and reserve the oil and butter for sautéing the shrimp.

In a large skillet, heat about 2 to 3 tablespoons of the reserved oil and then sauté the shrimp for about 5 minutes. Turn over very briefly and then remove. Add more oil as necessary to sauté all the shrimp. Salt to taste. Garnish with garlic bits and parsley. Serve with Mexican Rice.

Try brushing garlic oil over French bread, then sprinkling it with parsley and toasting it.

Serve this with the shrimp and accompany the dish with a lettuce and tomato salad.

Shrimp in Mustard Cream Sauce

1 pound large shrimp

2 tablespoons vegetable oil

1 shallot, minced

3 tablespoons dry white wine

1/2 cup heavy cream or whipping cream

1 tablespoon Dijon mustard with seed

Salt, to taste

Shell and devein shrimp. In a 10-inch skillet over medium heat cook shallot in hot oil for 5 minutes, stirring often. Increase heat to medium-high. Add shrimp. Cook 5 minutes or until shrimp turns pink, stirring often. Remove shrimp to bowl. Add wine to drippings in skillet. Cook over medium heat for 2 minutes. Add cream and mustard. Cook for 2 minutes. Return shrimp to skillet. Stir until heated through. Salt to taste.

Serve over hot, cooked rice.

Serves 4.

Gazpacho

Ingredients

- 2 cloves garlic
- 1/2 red onion
- 5 Roma tomatoes
- 2 stalks celery
- 1 large cucumber
- 1 zucchini
- 1/4 cup extra-virgin olive oil
- 2 tablespoons red wine vinegar
- 2 tablespoons sugar Several dashes hot sauce Dash salt
- Dash black pepper
- 4 cups good-quality tomato juice
- 1 pound shrimp, peeled and deveined Avocado slices, for serving
- hard-boiled eggs, finely minced Fresh cilantro leaves, for serving Crusty bread, for serving

Directions

Mince up the garlic, cut the onion into slices, and dice up the tomatoes, celery, cucumber and zucchini. Throw all the garlic, all the onion, half of the remaining diced vegetables and the oil into the bowl of a food processor or, if you like, a blender.

Splash in the vinegar and add the sugar, hot sauce, salt and pepper. Finally pour in 2 cups of the tomato juice and blend well. You'll basically have a tomato base with a beautiful confetti of vegetables.

Pour the blended mixture into a large bowl and add in the other half of the diced vegetables. Stir it together. Then stir in the remaining 2 cups tomato juice. Give it a taste and make sure the seasoning is right. Adjust as needed. Refrigerate for an hour if possible.

Grill or saute the shrimp until opaque. Set aside. Ladle the soup into bowls, add the grilled shrimp and garnish with avocado slices, egg and cilantro leaves. Serve with crusty bread on the side.

Shrimp Linguine Alfredo

1 (12 ounce) package linguine pasta

1/4 cup butter, melted

4 tablespoons diced onion

4 teaspoons minced garlic

40 small shrimp, peeled and deveined

1 cup half-and-half

2 teaspoons ground black pepper

6 tablespoons grated Parmesan cheese

4 sprigs fresh parsley

4 slices lemon, for garnish

Cook pasta in a large pot of boiling water until al dente; drain. Meanwhile, melt butter in a large saucepan. Saute onion and garlic over medium heat until tender. Add shrimp; saute over high heat for 1 minute, stirring constantly. Stir in half-and-half. Cook, stirring constantly, until sauce thickens. Place pasta in a serving dish, and cover with shrimp sauce. Sprinkle with black pepper and Parmesan cheese. Garnish with parsley and lemon slices.

Shrimp Marinara

1 (16 oz.) can of tomatoes, cut up

2 tbsp. minced parsley

1 clove garlic, minced

1/2 tsp. dried basil

1 tsp. salt

1/4 tsp. pepper

1 tsp. dried oregano

1 (6 oz.) can tomato paste

1/2 tsp. seasoned salt

1 lb. cooked shelled shrimp

Grated Parmesan cheese

Cooked spaghetti

In a crock pot, combine tomatoes with parsley, garlic, basil, salt, pepper, oregano, tomato paste, and seasoned salt. Cover and cook on low for 6 to 7 hours.

Turn control to high, stir in shrimp, cover and cook on high for 10 to 15 minutes more. Serve over cooked spaghetti.

Top with Parmesan cheese.

Shrimp Newburg

1 pound shrimp, cooked, deveined

1 (4 ounce can mushrooms

3 hard-boiled eggs, peeled and chopped

1/2 cup Parmesan cheese

4 tablespoons butter

1/2 onion, chopped

1 clove garlic, chopped

6 tablespoons flour

3 cups milk

4 tablespoons dry sherry

Worcestershire sauce

Salt and pepper

Tabasco sauce

Preheat oven to 375 degrees F.

Melt butter and then sauté the onion and garlic until tender. Add the flour. Mix well. Gradually add the milk, stirring constantly. Cook until the sauce thickens. Add the sherry and the seasonings to taste.

In a separate bowl, combine shrimp, mushrooms, eggs, and parsley. Add sauce along with 1/4 cup cheese to shrimp mixture. Mix well.

Pour the mixture into a 2-quart casserole dish and top with remaining cheese. Dot with the butter.

Bake 10 minutes, until slightly browned on top.

Spicy Marinated Shrimp

2 lbs. Large shrimp, peeled and deveined

1 Teaspoon Salt

1 Lemon, cut in half

8 Cup Water

Cup White wine vinegar or tarragon vinegar

Cup Olive oil

1-2 Serrano chiles (more or less, depending on taste), seeds and veins removed, finely minced

$\frac{1}{4}$ Cup Fresh cilantro, chopped

2 Large cloves garlic, minced or put through a garlic press

2 Teaspoon Fresh cilantro, chopped (if desired)

3 Green onions (white part only), minced

Freshly ground black pepper, to taste

Combine the water, salt and lemon halves in a Dutch oven, and bring to a boil. Add the shrimp, stir, and boil gently for 4–5 minutes. Remove from heat and drain.

Combine the vinegar, olive oil, chiles, cilantro and garlic in a large zip-top plastic bag or other plastic container. Add the boiled shrimp, and refrigerate for 12 hours or overnight, turning several times.

To serve, drain liquid from shrimp. In a large bowl, combine chilled shrimp with additional cilantro, green onions and black pepper, and toss well. Arrange in a serving dish, and serve immediately.

Spicy Singapore Shrimp

2 pounds large shrimp (Parr recommends head-on shrimp)

2 tablespoons ketchup

3 tablespoons Sriracha

2 tablespoons lemon juice

2 tablespoons soy sauce

1 tablespoon sugar

2 medium jalapeños, seeded and minced

white bulb of 1 stalk of lemongrass, minced

1 tablespoon fresh ginger, minced

4 scallions, sliced thinly

1/4 cup cilantro, chopped

Combine the ketchup, vinegar (if using), chili sauce, lemon juice, soy sauce and sugar.

In a large skillet, heat up a little vegetable oil and cook the shrimp on high heat. When they start to turn pink, flip them.
Add a little bit more oil and the jalapeños, garlic, lemongrass and ginger. Stir often until the mixture is heated through. Warning: it will smell delicious. Try not to lose your focus.

Stir-fry the scallions and the ketchup mixture in the skillet for 30 seconds, then mix in the chopped cilantro. Serve the shrimp with rice.

Starlight Shrimp

- 6 cups of water
- 2 tbsp. salt
- 1 lemon, halved
- 1 stalk celery, cut into 3 inch pieces
- 2 bay leaves
- A dash of cayenne pepper
- 1/4 cup parsley, minced
- 1 package Zatarains Crawfish/Crab/Shrimp boil (if available)
- 2 lbs. unpeeled shrimp freshly trolled in Mobile Bay
- 1 container of cocktail sauce

Slice off heads of shrimp.

Combine first 8 ingredients in a large pot or Dutch Oven. Bring to boil. Add shrimp in shells and cook about 5 minutes until they become pink. Drain well with cold water and chill.

Peel and devein shrimp, then store in chilled cooler.

Zesty Alabama Cocktail Sauce

- 2/3 cup chili sauce
- 1/4 cup lemon juice
- 2 to 3 tbsp. prepared horseradish
- 2 tsp. Worcestershire sauce
- 1/4 tsp. hot sauce

Mix all ingredients together. Sample and add to your taste. The more, the zestier! Store in chilled cooler.

Carry the cooler to the beach and, as the sun fades over the Gulf waters and Jimmy Buffett's rendition of "Stars Fell On Alabama" plays softly in the background, enjoy the shrimp, perhaps with a glass of wine or beer.

Butterfly Shrimp

- 1 lb. extra-large shrimp
- 4 slices bacon
- 1 large onion
- 1 garlic clove
- 2 eggs
- 4 Tbsp. flour
- 2 cups vegetable oil

For sauce:

- 1/4 cup catsup
- 2 Tbsp. Worcestershire sauce
- 3 Tbsp. sugar
- Dash pepper
- 1/2 cup water
- 2 Tbsp. cornstarch
- 2 Tbsp. water
- 1 Tbsp. oil
- 1/2 tsp. salt

Shell, devein and butterfly shrimp. Cut bacon into 1-1/2 inch pieces. Slice onion and saute in oil. Crush garlic. Place slice of bacon over each shrimp. Lay on platter. Beat eggs. Add flour to eggs and beat with wire whisk until batter thickens. Holding shrimp and bacon together dip in batter and place into hot oil for 2-3 minutes. Remove and drain on paper towels. Set aside.

In small bowl mix catsup, Worcestershire sauce, sugar, pepper and water. In a cup blend cornstarch and water. Heat oil and add crushed garlic and salt until golden brown. Add to this the catsup mixture and bring ingredients to a boil. Stir in cornstarch until mixture thickens. Serve shrimp over onions and spoon sauce over shrimp.

Cajun Shrimp

(2 servings)

- 1 lb. shrimp (3-4 inch w/out heads)
- 1/4 tsp. cayenne
- 1 tsp. black pepper
- 1/2 tsp. salt
- 1/2 tsp. red chile pepper flakes
- 1/2 tsp. thyme
- 1/2 tsp. rosemary
- 1/8 tsp. oregano
- 3 Tbsp. butter
- 1 1/2 tsp. garlic, minced
- 1 tsp. Worcestershire sauce
- 1/2 cup beer (room temperature)

Shell, de-vein, and rinse shrimp. Grind seasonings in mortar and pestle. In large skillet over high heat, melt butter; add garlic, seasonings, and Worcestershire sauce. When bubbly, add shrimp. Cook 2 minutes, stirring and shaking the skillet. Add beer and cook 3 minutes. Remove shrimp and reduce sauce, adjusting seasoning. Serve shrimp over rice with sauce spooned over the top.

Chilled Aromatic Shrimp with Cilantro-Ginger-Lime Cream

- 1 cup loosely packed fresh cilantro
- 1 tablespoon fresh ginger, chopped
- 2 cloves garlic
- 2 scallions (green onions), sliced
- 1 jalapeno pepper, halved and seeded
- 1 teaspoon sugar
- One-half teaspoon salt
- 3 tablespoons mild vegetable oil
- 3 tablespoons fresh lime juice
- 1 to 2 pounds medium or large shrimps peeled but with tails left on.
- 1 cup heavy cream

In a food processor, combine cilantro, ginger, garlic, scallions, jalapeno, and process until finely chopped (or chop fine by hand). Add sugar, salt, oil and lime juice and mix well. Toss Shrimp in mixture until well-coated; cover bowl and let stand an hour at cool room temperature or longer in the refrigerator.

Spoon shrimps out of marinade and sauté lightly (without additional oil) until shrimps are barely cooked. Arrange on serving plate and chill.

Add reserved marinade to the liquid from the cooked shrimp and voil, stirring, until the liquid evaporates, leaving a thick green puree. Add cream and boil again, stirring constantly, until thick enough to pour. Do not reduce too much; this sauce thickens considerably as it cools. Pour sauce into a serving bowl and refrigerate with the shrimp until both are well-chilled and ready to serve.

New Orleans BBQ shrimp

- 1 c (2 sticks) margarine
- 1/2 c vegetable oil
- 1/2 c chicken broth (canned is fine)
- 4 t finely minced garlic
- 5 whole bay leaves, torn into pieces
- 4 t dried rosemary, crushed
- 1 t dried sweet basil
- 1 t greek oregano
- 1 t dried thyme
- 1/2 t salt
- 1/2 t (or more) cayenne pepper
- 4 t paprika
- 1 1/2 t freshly ground black pepper
- 1 T fresh lemon juice
- 2 lb whole fresh shrimp in the shell (with heads if possible)

In a heavy sauté pan or saucepan melt the margarine, then add the oil and mix well. Add all the other ingredients except the shrimp and broth, and cook over medium heat, stirring constantly, until the sauce begins to boil. Reduce the heat to low and simmer for 7 to 8 minutes, stirring frequently, then remove the pan from the heat and let it stand, uncovered, at room temperature for at least 30 minutes. Add the shrimp to the sauce, mix thoroughly, and put the pan back on the burner. Cook over medium heat for

6 to 8 minutes or just until the shrimp turn pink. Add the broth, shaking the pan back and forth to mix. Preferably, place the pan into a preheated 450 deg F oven and bake for 10 minutes. OR simmer loosely covered on the stovetop for about 5 or 10 minutes. Serve equal portions of shrimp with about 1/2 c of the sauce ladled over each one. You will need bibs and lots of bread to sop up the sauce. Also, fingers are a necessary eating utensil. A good side dish is quartered red new potatoes, baked in olive oil, lemon juice, salt, pepper, and several bay leaves. A green salad and bread finishes the meal. Makes 5 generous (nearly 1/2 lb) servings

Curried Corn and Shrimp Soup

2 cups regular-strength chicken broth

2 medium-size tart apples (peeled, cored and chopped)

1 large onion (chopped)

1/2 tsp curry powder
1 large red bell pepper (stemmed and seeded)

4 cups cold buttermilk

1/4 cup lime juice

1 1/2 cups cooked corn kernels

1/2 cup minced fresh cilantro

1/3 lb. tiny cooked shrimp

Cilantro Sprigs (optional)

In a 4- to 5- quart pan over high heat combine broth, apples, onion, and curry. Cover and bring to a boil, then simmer until apples mash easily (about

30 min). Let cool, then cover and chill until cold, at least 3 hours or up to a day. Smoothly puree mixture in a blender or food processor.

Cut a few thin slivers from bell pepper and set aside; dice remaining pepper and put into a tureen with apple puree, buttermilk, lime juice, 1 1/4 cups of corn and minced cilantro. Ladle soup into bowls and top with shrimp, remaining corn, bell pepper strips, and cilantro sprigs.

Fiesta Shrimp

- Clean & devein 1 lb shrimp (enough for 2, 4, etc people)

In a wok (on medium to medium high), add:

- 1 TBS butter

When melted, add

- Shrimp
- garlic to taste (I like a lot of garlic so I would put in several cloves chopped finely or put through a garlic press - if you're lazy you can buy jars of minced garlic)

Stir quickly till all shrimp has turned pink Add 1 cup fresh corn (or thawed frozen) Stir quickly to heat through

- Add 1 cup salsa (I prefer hot - choose your own strength)

Stir quickly to heat thoroughly

Serve with Black beans, fresh tossed salad with crumbled blue cheese & warm flour or wheat tortillas

Pasta with Shrimp in Tomato Cream

- 1/3 cup dried tomatoes packed in oil, drained, reserve oil, and slivered. 1 clove garlic, minced or pressed
- 1 lb large (31-35/lb) shrimp, shelled, deveined 1/4 cup thinly sliced green onions, including tops 1 1/2 Tbs chopped fresh basil, or 1 tsp dried basil 1/4 tsp white pepper
- 1 cup chicken broth
- 3/4 cup dry vermouth
- 1 cup whipping cream
- 10 oz linguine
- garnish: grated parmesan cheese and/or fresh basil sprigs

Add 2 Tbs oil from tomatoes, heat in wide frying pan over medium-high heat. Add garlic and shrimp when oil is hot. Cook, while stirring, until shrimp are opaque when cut (about 6 min). Remove from pan. Add onions, chopped basil, tomatoes, pepper, broth vermouth and cream to pan. Boil over high hear, stirring occasionally until reduced to about 1 1/2 cups (about 10 min). Return shrimp to pan and stir until just heated through.

Meanwhile cook linguine in 3 qts boiling water until just al dente (about 8 min for dried linguine).

Drain, arrange on 4 plates and spoon sauce over.
Garnish with basil, cheese to taste.

Caribbean Coconut Shrimp

1 lb shrimp - peeled and deveined

Batter
3/4 cup flour
1 egg
1/2 Tbsp baking powder
1/2 cup beer

Coating
1/4 cup flour
1 1/2 cups dried grated coconut
1 Tbsp salt
1/2 Tbsp ground black pepper
1/2 Tbsp cayenne (or ground chilis)
1/2 Tbsp paprika
1 Tbsp garlic powder(not Garlic salt!)
1/2 tsp dried thyme
1/2 tsp oregano

Dip shrimp individually into the batter and then roll in the coating.
Deep-fry.
Allow to drain on paper towel.

Serve with various dips: eg. honey + soy sauce + tobacco; honey + mustard or marmalade + ginger.

Papaya garlic Shrimp

In a saucepan melt 3 Tbsp butter, saute 2 cloves of garlic (chopped, not crushed) and half a cooking onion (actually, spanish onion is better), once the garlic has browned and the onion has cleared, add half a papaya chopped into 1/2 inch chunks and a tsp of dried thyme leaves, stir until papaya just starts to go mushy. Dump all of this into a bowl and then sauté your shrimp in the same saucepan (with a little more butter) for a couple of minutes. Finally, throw the papaya/garlic/onion mixture back in for another 5 min on low heat. Serve over rice or with thai noodles or what have you.

Shrimp Creole

- 2 lbs baby shrimp
- 3 T butter
- 1 C onions, chopped coarsly
- 1 C green pepper, chopped
- 1 C chopped zucchini
- 1 C chopped celery
- 2 cloves garlic, pressed
- 4 large tomatoes, chopped
- 8 oz tomato sauce
- 1/2 tsp pepper
- 2 tsp shredded fresh lemon peel
- 1/16 tsp cloves
- 1 bay leaf
- 1 tsp thyme
- 1 tsp honey
- 3T parsley

In a large saucepan, sauté onion, green pepper, zucchini, and celery till tender in butter. Add garlic & tomatoes, bring to a boil. Reduce heat & add tomato sauce, pepper, lemon peel, cloves, bay, thyme, and honey. Simmer 15-20 minutes, stir frequently. Stir in shrimp & heat thoroughly. Serve over hot rice. Add hot pepper sauce if desired.

Shrimp and Grits/Classic Charleston Breakfast Shrimp

"This is what most Charlestonians think of as shrimp and grits. The secret to a nonpasty gravy is to cook the flour, which takes about 5 minutes. Even the largest shrimp need only cook for 3 minutes."

- 1 cup (1/2 pound) peeled shrimp
- 2 T (1/8 c) fresh lemon juice
- salt and cayenne pepper to taste
- 3 T bacon grease
- 1 small onion, finely chopped (about 1/4 c) about 1/4 c finely chopped green bell pepper 2 T (1/8 c) unbleached all-purpose flour
- 3/4 to 1 c hot water or stock (shrimp, chicken, or vegetable)
- Grits

In a bowl, sprinkle the shrimp with lemon juice, salt, and cayenne and set aside. Heat the bacon grease in a skillet and saute the onion and pepper over medium heat until the onion begins to become transparent, about 10 min. Sprinkle the flour over the vegetables and stir constantly for about 2 min, until the flour begins to brown.

Add the shrimp and about 3/4 c of water or stock, stirring constantly and turning the shrimp so that they cook evenly. Cook for another 2 to 3 minutes, until the shrimp are cooked through and the gravy is uniformly smooth, thinning with a little extra water or stock if necessary. Serve immediately over the grits.

Biscuit Topped Seafood Gumbo Pie

Gumbo:

- 3 tablespoons plus 1 teaspoon vegetable oil
- 3 tablespoons all-purpose flour
- 3 tablespoons butter
- 3/4 pound smoked sausage, sliced
- 3/4 pound cooked boneless ham steak, cut into 2 by 1/4 inch strips
- 1 large onion, chopped
- 2 garlic cloves, minced
- 1/2 green bell pepper, chopped
- 1/2 red bell pepper, chopped
- 1 small celery rib, minced
- 3 tablespoons rice
- 2 cups chicken stock
- 2 teaspoons fresh lemon juice
- 1/2 teaspoon cayenne pepper
- 3/4 pound shrimp, shelled
- 1/2 pound okra, sliced
- salt and freshly ground black pepper

Biscuit topping:

- 2 cups all-purpose flour
- 1 tablespoon baking powder
- 2 teaspoons sugar
- 1/2 teaspoon baking soda

- 1/2 teaspoon salt
- 6 1/2 tablespoons cold butter
- 3/4 cup buttermilk

Make the gumbo: In a heavy medium skillet, combine 3 tablespoons of the oil with the flour and cook over moderately low heat, stirring occasionally, until the roux is dark mahogany in color, about 1 hour. Do not let burn. Immediately remove from heat. In a medium flameproof casserole, melt 2 tablespoons of the butter with the Remaining 1 teaspoon oil. Add the sliced sausage and cook over moderate heat until well browned, about 5 minutes. Transfer to a plate with a slotted spoon. Add the ham strips to the casserole and cook until lightly browned, about 7 minutes; add to the plate with the sausage slices.

Add the remaining 1 tablespoon butter and the onion to the casserole. Cook over moderate heat, stirring constantly, until softened and translucent, about 2 minutes. Reduce the heat to moderately low and add the garlic

Creamy butter shrimp

- 1/2 oz. Parmigiano Reggiano) grated
- 2 tbsp. Almond Flour
- 1/2 tsp. Baking Powder
- 1/4 tsp. Curry Powder
- 1 tbsp. Water
- 1 large Egg
- 12 medium Shrimp
- 3 tbsp. Coconut Oil

Creamy Butter Sauce

- 2 tbsp. Unsalted Butter
- 1/2 small Onion, diced
- 1 clove Garlic, finely chopped
- 2 small Thai Chilies, sliced

Garnish

- 2 tbsp. Curry Leaves
- 1/2 cup Heavy Cream
- 1/3 oz. Mature Cheddar
- Salt and Pepper to Taste
- 1/8 tsp. Sesame Seeds

1. Remove the shells of the shrimps but leave the tail part if you'd like
2. Pat the cleaned shrimps dry with paper towels.
3. In a bowl, add 0.5 oz. grated Parmigiano Reggiano, 2 tbsp. almond flour, 1/2 tsp. baking powder and 1/4 tsp.

curry powder (optional). Mix well. Gently cut the surface of the shrimps and devein. Clean well Into the mixture, add in 1 egg and 1 tbsp. water. Mix well until smooth.

4. Preheat a pan on medium heat. Add in 3 tsbp. coconut oil. Once the oil is hot, generously coat the shrimps with the batter and pan-fry the shrimps. Do these two to three at a time.

5. Wait until the shrimps turn golden brown and then remove them from the pan. Put on a cooling rack. Pan-fry extra batter if any left.

6. Preheat a pan to medium-low heat. Add in 2 tbsp. unsalted butter. Once the butter has melted, add in 1/2 chopped onion.

7. Wait until the onion turns translucent and then add in finely chopped garlic, sliced Thai chilies and 2 tbps. Curry leaves. Stir-fry everything until fragrant.

8. Add in the battered shrimp and coat well with the sauce.

9. Garnish with sesame seeds and serve! Goes well with cauliflower fried rice.

Prosciutto wrapped shrimp

- 10 oz. Pre-Cooked Shrimp
- 11 slices Prosciutto
- 1/3 cup Blackberries, Ground
- 1/3 cup Red Wine
- 2 tbsp. Olive Oil
- 1 tbsp. Mint Leaves, Chopped
- 1-2 tbsp. NOW Erythritol (to taste)

THE EXECUTION

1. Preheat your oven to 425F. Slice prosciutto in half or in thirds, depending on how many shrimp you have and their size. Wrap shrimp in prosciutto, starting from the tail and working your way up. Lay on a baking sheet, drizzle with 2 tbsp. olive oil, and cook for 15 minutes.

2. In a spice grinder, grind 1/3 cup Blackberries.

3. In a pan, add the blackberry puree and mint leaves. Add 1-2 tbsp. erythritol, to your tastes, then let cook for 2-3 minutes.

Add 1/3 cup red wine to the sauce and mix well. Then let reduce under simmer. Taste when reduced and add more sweetener if needed.

Serve with sauce on the side or drizzled over!

This will make about 4 single servings.
Each serving comes out to 247 Calories, 12.8g Fats, 1g Net Carbs, and 13.8g Protein

Thai peanut shrimp curry

- 2 tbsp. Green Curry Paste
- 1 cup Vegetable Stock
- 1 cup Coconut Milk
- 6 oz. Precooked Shrimp
- 5 oz. Broccoli Florets
- 3 tbsp. Cilantro, chopped
- 2 tbsp. Coconut Oil
- 1 tbsp. Peanut Butter
- 1 tbsp. Soy Sauce (or coconut Aminos)
- Juice of 1/2 Lime
- 1 medium Spring Onion, chopped
- 1 tsp. Crushed Roasted Garlic
- 1 tsp. Minced Ginger
- 1 tsp. Fish Sauce
- 1/2 tsp. Turmeric
- 1/4 tsp. Xanthan Gum
- 1/2 cup Sour Cream (for topping)

THE EXECUTION

1. Start by adding 2 tbsp. coconut oil in a pan over medium heat.

2. When the coconut oil is melted and the pan is hot, add the 1 tsp. Roasted garlic, 1 tsp. minced ginger, and 1 spring onion (chopped). Allow to cook for about a minute, then add 1 tbsp. green curry paste, and 1/2 tsp. turmeric.

3. Add 1 tbsp. soy sauce (or coconut Aminos), 1 tsp. fish sauce, and 1 tbsp. peanut butter to the pan and mix together well.

4. Add 1 cup of vegetable stock and 1 cup of coconut milk (from the carton). Stir well and then add another 1 tbsp. green curry paste.

5. Let simmer for a few minutes. In the meantime, measure out 6 oz. pre- cooked shrimp.

6. Add 1/4 tsp. xanthan gum to the curry and mix well.

7. Once your curry begins thickening up a little bit, add the broccoli florets and stir well.

8. Chop 3 tbsp. fresh cilantro and add to the pan.

9. Finally, once you are happy with the consistency of the curry, add the shrimp and lime juice from 1/2 lime, and mix everything together.

10. Let simmer for a few minutes. Taste and season with salt and pepper if needed.

11. Serve! You can stir in 1/4 cup of sour cream per serving.